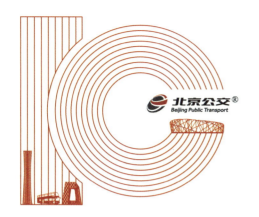

岁月无声，时光有痕。根植红色基因的北京公交，在新时代的征程中砥砺前行，以改革创新蓄力发展，迎来了连续发布社会责任报告的第十个年头。十载风雨，北京公交与首都同心同行，携一路荣光，载万千期盼，穿梭流动，不舍昼夜，流淌着民生的温度，镌刻着城市的变化。一辆公交车，一路为人民。一张线路图，方寸有乾坤。北京公交载着责任印记继续出发，将车辆串联成更密集的线网，把站台叠加成更立体的场站，让时间和空间交织流转，充盈着感动，驶向可持续发展的美好未来。

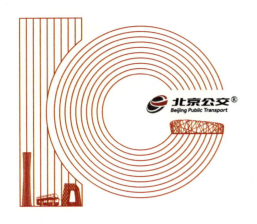

目录 CONTENTS

24
十年：思变求新，笃行致远
26 十年前行，满载责任
34 十年变革，发展为民

04 卷首语
06 我们的问候
08 走进北京公交
16 社会责任管理

44
服务：民之所需，行之所至
46 密织线网畅通城市脉动
47 更多出行选择
47 公交先行赋能一体化发展
50 数字转型，智慧出行
51 每一站，与平安相伴
57 让你我乐享其"乘"

86

未来：一路同行，向可持续

88 | 怀着初心出发，启航美好出行
89 | 并肩同行，共赴精彩
90 | 城市更新，让"老地方"焕发新活力
91 | 打造标准化建设新高地
92 | 领跑自动驾驶新赛道
94 | 建设新型公交智库
96 | 可持续的公交，可持续的未来

98 | 展望
100 | 关键绩效
102 | 指标索引
103 | 关于本报告

68

共享：携手并进，同创价值

70 | 成就每个人的价值
77 | 环境友好，绿色出行
80 | 为社区留下长久感动
83 | 共托乡村振兴新希望

60

担当：方向盘上，用心坚守

62 | 冰雪映照下的冬奥保障
64 | 护航每一次重大活动
65 | 同心协力抗击疫情

奋进十年，以绿色为底色

环境友好型公交引领清洁出行新风尚

奋进十年，以共享为胸怀

开辟城乡均等化、区域一体化发展新格局

回首与展望间

宏伟蓝图已徐徐展开

奔赴新征程

北京公交步履必将更加坚定

与乘客同频，持续优化服务供给

与时代共振，探求招新公交价值

与智慧同轴，推进创新驱动发展

与行业共转，引领构建产业生态

与利益相关方对话，共建发展共同体

携手并进，砥砺前行

打造更人本友好、更便捷通畅、更灵活多样的公共交通

共赢更加美好、更可持续的未来

交通天下，大道致远

北京公交与您一路同心同行

卷首语

日升月落

冬去春来

从2013到2022，新时代的十年里

北京公交始终与责任偕行

驶过道路万千

历经大战大考

一车一线，一里一程

镌刻着出行之变、城市之变、时代之变

记述着让更多人享受更好公共出行服务的使命愿景

奋进十年，以民心为初心

高品质多元公交服务提升公众出行幸福感

奋进十年，以责任为担当

圆满完成历次重大政治活动运输保障任务

奋进十年，以创新为引擎

数字化转型催生高质量发展新动能

我们的问候

十年栉风沐雨，十年春华秋实。

2013年，习近平总书记提出"发展公共交通是现代城市发展的方向"。党中央、国务院先后印发了《交通强国建设纲要》《国家综合立体交通网规划纲要》，强调优先发展城市公共交通，深入实施公交优先战略，为公共交通的发展指明了道路和方向。着眼"十四五"，北京市委市政府进一步赋予了北京公交发展新定位和新要求——"打造现代城市客运出行综合服务商"，推动城市客运出行综合服务、汽车服务与贸易两大主业协同发展。

这十年，我们在习近平新时代中国特色社会主义思想指引下，在市委市政府的坚强领导下，凝心聚力，砥砺奋进，完成十年全面深化改革任务目标，企业治理体系和治理能力现代化水平全面提升。这十年，我们把创新作为引领发展的第一动力，始终摆在企业发展全局的核心地位，不断创新理念、创新模式、创新服务，实现了地面公交出行服务人性化、个性化、数字化、智能化的跨越式发展。这十年，我们以乘客为本，持续向利益相关方赋能，与责任偕行，连续十年披露社会责任报告，谱写了大国首都地面公共交通履责实践的辉煌篇章。

定格瞬间，洞见十年。我们坚定不移与党的旗帜同行、与党的使命同向、与党的号令同频。铭记国企责任担当，义不容辞为政治任务和重大活动护航,圆满完成新中国成立70周年庆祝活动、中国共产党建党100周年大会、北京冬奥会和冬残奥会等交通服务保障任务。我们迎来建企百年,回首致敬峥嵘岁月,编纂《北京公交百年志》和制作企业发展百集微视频,圆满举办建企100周年文艺演出活动,传承薪火,接续奋斗。面对突如其来的新冠肺炎疫情,我们坚持人民至上和生命至上,周密部署,科学防控,开展全员核酸检测,对所有运营车辆、场站定时消毒,采取大站快车、区间车等调度措施,上下同心、共克时艰,保证首都地面公交安全有序运行。

守正创新,真情服务。我们牢牢把握和坚定践行"让更多的人享受更好的公共出行服务"的企业使命,深入优化公交线网布局,全力推进数字化转型,大力实施区域智能调度改革,持续探索业务模式创新,贯彻落实京津冀协同发展战略,不断满足人民对美好出行的需要。2022年,首都公交专用道增加至1005车道公里,京开高速、三环路、京藏高速、京港澳高速等公交专用道基本成网;北京公交常规公交线路长度增至30173.9公里,近200条干线构成了"棋盘+环+放射"的地面公交骨架网络结构;通过智能调度,车次兑现率达到99%以上,发车准点率达到98%以上;定制公交线路达418条(区位),通勤时间节省了30%以上;运营雄安新区公交线路总长度347.1公里,走深走实京津冀协同发展战略。

生态优先,绿色发展。我们深刻认识和坚决贯彻习近平总书记提出的"绿水青山就是金山银山"理念,积极践行碳达峰碳中和行动,以双碳"1+N"政策体系为遵循,推动绿色低碳发展。加速老旧公交车辆淘汰,推进绿色低碳装备更新,加强充电桩、加氢站、智能电子站牌等配套设施建设。2022年,北京公交清洁能源和新能源公交车占比达94.27%,建设完成2座加氢站和225处公交场站内1524台充电桩。全面推行清洁生产,严格管控碳排放,积极开展碳排放交易,2022年,北京公交碳排放交易共计11.41万吨,净收益达1165.02万元。

勇立潮头,敢为人先。我们深刻领悟"创新是引领发展的第一动力",坚持创新驱动,以敢闯敢试、敢为人先的精神不断向新兴领域探索,在多个方面开启公交行业先河。提出"出行即生活"新理念,让公交不仅是运载的工具,更是移动的生活场景,绘制"城市移动会客厅"新蓝图。着眼自动驾驶前沿科技和未来智能交通发展战略布局,与丰田公司在首钢园区合作试点自动驾驶载客运营,与北汽福田等产学研组织合作开展自动驾驶公交示范项目。成功设立全国公交行业首个博士后科研工作站,引进第一批博士后研究人员,建设具有全球视野、走在世界前列的新型公交智库,加速公交企业从劳动密集型向高新技术密集型转变。

守望相助,命运与共。我们始终与利益相关方携手同行,共创共享发展成果。坚持"人才强企"战略,多措并举推动员工职业教育和人才培养,成就每个人的价值。持续加强适老化改造,提升无障碍出行服务水平,2022年,北京公交配备低地板车辆1.4万余辆,其中带有无障碍导板的车辆1.2万余辆,城区无障碍公交车占比超过80%。助力河北、内蒙古、西藏、新疆、湖北等受援地区巩固拓展脱贫攻坚成果同乡村振兴有效衔接,有序推进北京密云区南沟村脱低增收和门头沟区斋堂镇3个集体经济薄弱村"消薄",增加山区线网覆盖,建设"村村通"公交,全面推进乡村振兴。携手全球范围内多个城市公交,将《北京宣言》共识转化为深刻实践,致力于打造一个紧密联系的公共交通发展共同体,共商共建更加人本友好、更加便捷通畅、更加舒适安全、更加节能环保、更加灵活多样的公共交通。

十年赓续谋蜕变,奋楫扬帆谱新篇。2023年是全面落实党的二十大精神的开局之年,也是"十四五"承上启下的关键一年。北京公交将延续新时代十年的铿锵脚步,锚定"十四五"发展目标和2035年远景目标,以奋斗之姿、实干之态,勇毅前行,努力打造国内领先、世界一流的现代城市客运出行综合服务商,不断提升乘客获得感、幸福感和安全感。

走进北京公交

关于我们

北京公共交通控股（集团）有限公司是以经营地面公共交通客运业务为依托，多元化投资，多种经济类型并存，集客运、汽车修理、旅游、汽车租赁、广告等为一体的国有独资大型公交企业集团。根据"十四五"发展规划，北京公交确立城市客运出行综合服务、汽车服务与贸易两大主业，立足首都，服务京津冀，努力打造国内领先、世界一流的现代城市客运出行综合服务商。

我们承担着北京地面公交的主体任务，在北京城市公共交通发展中发挥着重要作用。截至2022年底，北京公交总资产643.27亿元，净资产444.40亿元，共有员工84211人。运营车辆32783辆，其中，公共电汽车23465辆，清洁能源和新能源公交车比例达到94.27%。运营常规公交线路1291条，定制公交线路418条（区位），多样化公交专线158条。2022年公共电汽车行驶里程9.84亿公里，年客运量17.26亿人次。同时，运营2条现代有轨电车线路——西郊线和亦庄T1线。

城市客运出行综合服务

包括公共电汽车客运等客运出行服务、公交旅游、广告传媒和围绕客运出行开展的投融资和资产经营管理等

两大主业

汽车服务与贸易

包括汽车驾驶培训、汽车销售、汽车租赁、车辆维修和报废车辆拆解回收等

企业文化

使命

让更多的人享受更好的公共出行服务

愿景

引领公众出行方式,提升城市生活品质,成为国际知名的现代城市客运出行综合服务集团

核心价值观

以人为本 乘客至上 创新发展 追求卓越

企业精神

一心为乘客 服务最光荣
真情献社会 责任勇担当

组织机构

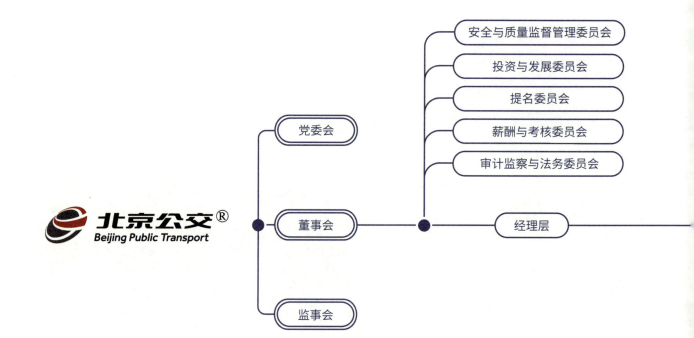

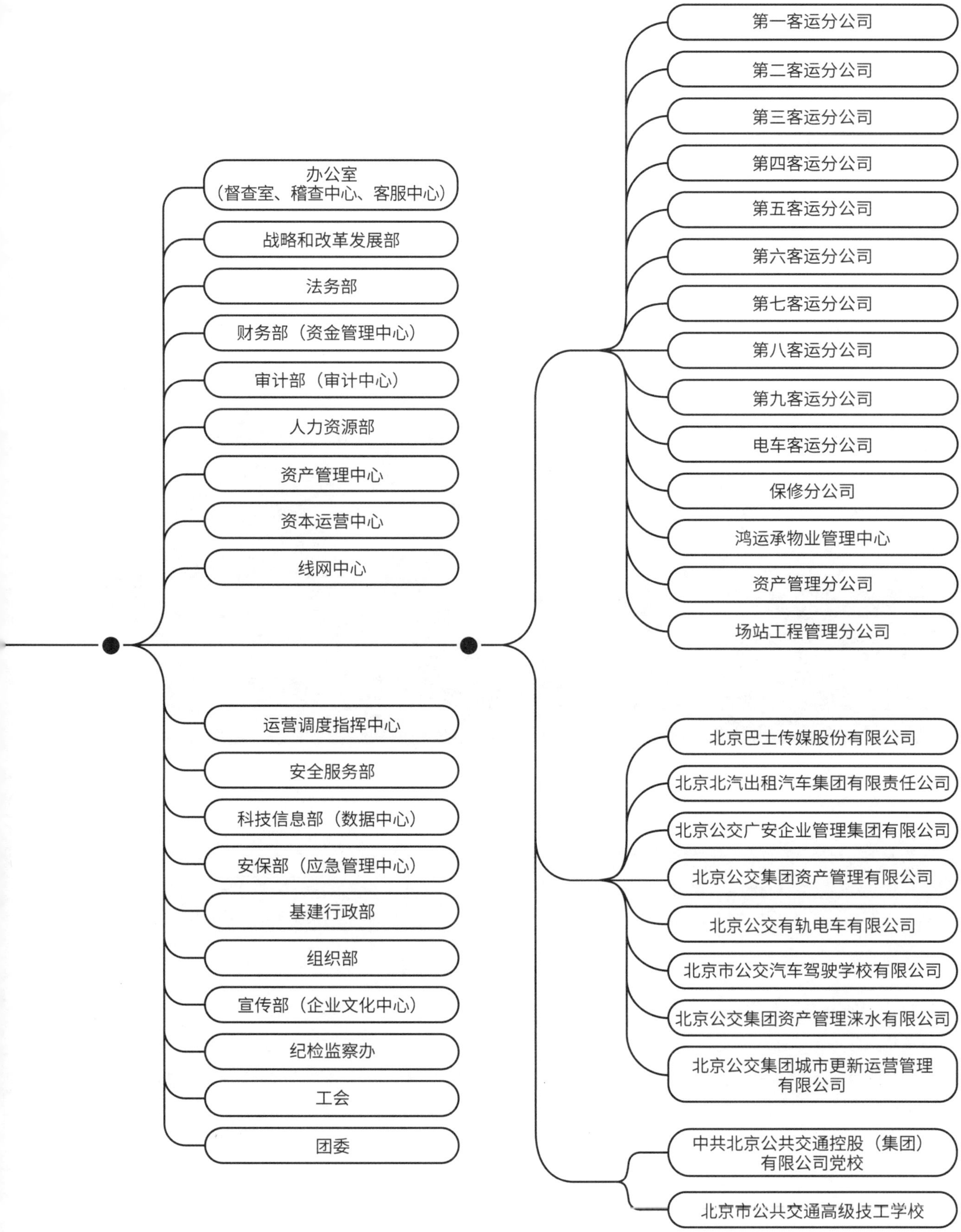

办公室
（督查室、稽查中心、客服中心）

战略和改革发展部

法务部

财务部（资金管理中心）

审计部（审计中心）

人力资源部

资产管理中心

资本运营中心

线网中心

运营调度指挥中心

安全服务部

科技信息部（数据中心）

安保部（应急管理中心）

基建行政部

组织部

宣传部（企业文化中心）

纪检监察办

工会

团委

第一客运分公司

第二客运分公司

第三客运分公司

第四客运分公司

第五客运分公司

第六客运分公司

第七客运分公司

第八客运分公司

第九客运分公司

电车客运分公司

保修分公司

鸿运承物业管理中心

资产管理分公司

场站工程管理分公司

北京巴士传媒股份有限公司

北京北汽出租汽车集团有限责任公司

北京公交广安企业管理集团有限公司

北京公交集团资产管理有限公司

北京公交有轨电车有限公司

北京市公交汽车驾驶学校有限公司

北京公交集团资产管理涞水有限公司

北京公交集团城市更新运营管理
有限公司

中共北京公共交通控股（集团）
有限公司党校

北京市公共交通高级技工学校

公司治理

北京公交牢牢坚持党的领导，深入推进治理体系与治理能力现代化，持续优化公司治理体系，强化制度与规范意识，坚持依法经营、合规经营、诚信经营，全面加强风险管控，为企业持续健康发展保驾护航。

党建领航

北京公交组织收看党的二十大开幕盛况

北京公交深刻牢记企业的政治责任，全面推进党建与企业中心工作深度融合。在党的二十大召开之年，我们在全系统开展全方位、多层次、立体化的深入学习，开展体现时代性、把握规律性、富于创造性的各类宣传，引导广大党员在深学细悟笃行上有更强自觉性，在学懂弄通做实上有更高要求，不断把学习引向深入，凝聚起奋进新征程、建功新时代的强大精神力量。

"全面从严治党永远在路上，党的自我革命永远在路上"。我们紧紧围绕"两个维护"，聚焦冬奥会冬残奥会、党的二十大会议等重大服务保障任务，强化政治监督。锲而不舍纠"四风"树新风，驰而不息加固中央八项规定精神堤坝，坚决打好作风建设攻坚战、持久战。把纪律建设摆在更加突出的位置，一体推进不敢腐、不能腐、不想腐，大力营造风清气正的良好政治生态。充分发挥"清风公交"和廉政教育基地平台作用，深入开展廉政宣传和警示教育，筑牢党员、干部拒腐防变的思想防线。

召开党委常委会

28 次

研究议题

227 项

党员

13413 人

党支部

375 个

开展党建活动

4212 次

党建培训时长

693 小时

全系统学习宣传贯彻党的二十大精神宣讲报告会

中国共产党北京公共交通控股(集团)有限公司第四次党员代表大会

治理机制

北京公交坚决贯彻落实"三重一大"决策制度,严格执行集团公司"第一议题"制度,编制《董事会授权决策方案》和《授权清单》,明确相关议事细则。同时指导各二级单位完善"一企一册"备案工作,逐步完善法人治理,提高治理体系和治理能力现代化水平。

召开董事会

7 次

董事会讨论议题

61 项

专委会研究议题

63 项

召开经理办公会

26 次

经理办公会讨论议题

221 项

扎实推进国企改革

北京公交深入贯彻落实国企改革三年行动重大决策部署,以踏石留印、抓铁有痕的韧劲,从公交发展的全过程、产业发展的全链条、企业发展的全生命周期出发,系统谋划,逐步完善集团公司人、财、物等资源配置,优化经营布局,促进降本增效,深化各领域、各层级改革,高质量完成6个方面99项重点改革任务,在深化改革中促进企业高质量发展,赋予企业新的生机活力,交出一份国企改革的亮眼"答卷"。北京公交在市国资委2021年度国企改革三年行动评估考核中被评为优秀,北京公交贯彻落实国企改革三年行动纪实宣传片荣登国务院国资委官网。

扫一扫,观看《坚定不移全面深化改革 奋力建设大国首都公交——北京公交集团贯彻落实国企改革三年行动纪实》宣传片

33家
应建董事会子企业

100%
实现外部董事占多数

一级企业及

51家
子企业

经理层成员任期制和契约化管理完成

100%
签约人数共计

131人

法治公交建设

北京公交始终牢记"心中信法、决策问法、经营用法、管理合法、改革有法"的法治公交精神,全面推进依法治企,切实防范合规风险。我们召开合规管理体系建设部署会,制发《北京公交集团合规管理体系建设实施方案》,按照"部署准备、试点实施、全面实施、总结提升"的"四步走"战略,推动构建全员参与、全程监控、全领域覆盖的合规管理体系。坚持流程管控,主动开展内控专项治理工作。持续完善知识产权管理。大力开展标准化建设,标准化三年行动计划圆满收官,高分通过国家级标准化试点终期评估验收,牵头修订北京市地方标准《公共汽车通用技术条件》并正式获批发布。

召开合规管理体系建设动员部署会

国家宪法日暨法治宣传周活动

标准化三年行动计划总结表彰大会

审计监督

北京公交优化审计模式方法及流程,推进审计向事前、事中和事后全过程监督转变。我们制定实施集团公司所属子企业内控监督评价"三年全覆盖"工作方案,聚焦重大决策落实、重点领域管控、重大资金使用等方面,精准高效全面推进落实,确保企业重点项目和资金投入使用的合规有效性。同时加强审计政策法规宣传教育,编发审计电子专刊4期、动态信息43期,营造了良好的审计文化氛围。2022年,完成审计项目76项、165分项次,上年度问题整改率99.1%,为企业改革和高质量发展提供了有力保障。

发布企业标准

27项

发布法治要闻

28篇

发布法治动态

67篇

发布法治公交企业微信

72篇

截至2022年底,累计

8件

发明专利获得授权

累计拥有实用新型专利

60件

社会责任管理

用心服务,责任先行。北京公交牢记公益性企业定位,知责于心,担责于身,履责于行,将社会责任理念融入企业发展战略,融入企业管理与日常运营,充分发挥企业核心优势,为经济、环境和社会的协调发展贡献力量,建立行之有效的社会责任管理体系,推动利益相关方沟通,为企业经营注入长久动力。

责任管理

北京公交高度重视社会责任管理工作,依靠权责清晰、运转有序的社会责任管理架构进行工作部署,进一步健全企业社会责任管理工作体系,形成由各专业社会责任编委、各二级单位通讯员构成的人员稳定、结构合理、工作高效的社会责任管理队伍。同时逐步规范社会责任报告编制、审议、发布、宣传以及利益相关方沟通访谈的工作流程,提高企业社会责任管理的工作效率和工作质量。

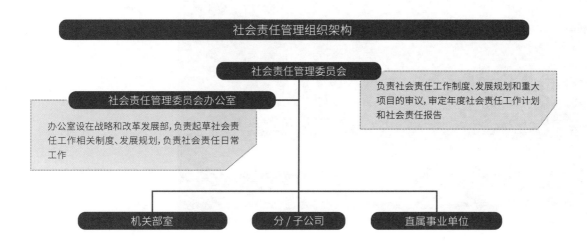

责任沟通

聆听不同群体的声音是北京公交履责践诺的开始。我们深刻认识自身所肩负的社会责任,通过实质性议题调研、交通开放日、公交爱好者见面会等方式,将报告打造成与利益相关方沟通交流的平台和媒介,树立并展示负责任、受尊重、可持续的窗口企业形象。

实质性议题

我们深入分析国内外社会责任标准和可持续发展宏观环境,对标行业社会责任先进企业,结合新时代北京公交的发展战略和"十四五"规划,遵照实质性、完整性和利益相关方参与原则,从"经济、环境和社会影响的重要性"和"对利益相关方评估和决策的影响"两个维度进行重要性排序,绘制实质性议题矩阵,让报告内容汇聚内外部群体的贡献和智慧,为社会责任报告编制和工作推进提供参考依据。

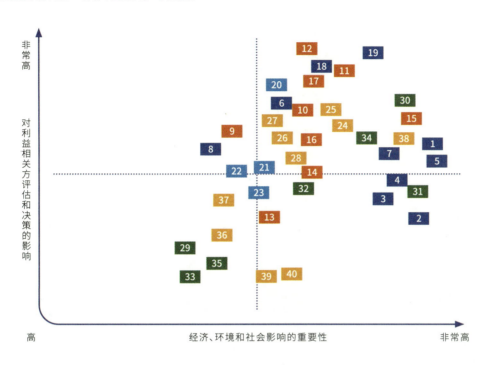

实质性议题矩阵

1.完善公司治理	11.公交服务便利性	21.提升应急管理能力	31.碳中和
2.加强党建	12.乘客满意度	22.强化安全管理	32.节能减排
3.依法治企	13.服务京津冀一体化	23.科技创安	33.绿色办公
4.贯彻宏观政策	14.科技创新	24.员工权益保护	34.应对气候变化
5.深化国企改革	15.数字化转型	25.平等雇佣	35.绿色环保公益
6.责任管理	16.重大活动和重要时期保障	26.职业健康管理	36.促进就业
7.党建引领	17.服务首都发展	27.员工培训与发展	37.乡村振兴
8.引领行业发展	18.保障乘客安全	28.员工关爱	38.应急救援
9.个性化服务	19.加强公共安全	29.倡导绿色出行	39.倡导文明出行
10.无障碍服务	20.培育安全文化	30.优化能源结构	40.志愿服务

注:2022年社会责任议题审核中,基于国内外社会责任发展趋势和时代热点,我们提升了议题5"深化国企改革"、议题15"数字化转型"的重要等级。

利益相关方沟通

我们积极开展多种形式、多样内容的沟通活动,借助多元平台,深入了解并积极回应各利益相关方对北京公交可持续发展的期望和诉求,与更多群体携手奔赴美好出行未来。

利益相关方	期望和诉求	回应方式
政府	守法合规 落实政府交通规划 服务区域经济发展 带动就业 响应疫情防控要求	合规运营与风险控制 依法纳税 主动接受政府监督 服务京津冀协同发展 常态化疫情防控
乘客	优质贴心服务 保障出行安全	提供多样化出行服务 促进无障碍服务 乘客满意度调查 接诉即办 驾驶员行车安全培训 安全应急管理
员工	员工权益保障 员工成长发展 关爱员工生活	完善薪酬福利体系 工会、职工代表大会 职业健康与安全管理 开展员工培训 困难员工帮扶
行业/合作伙伴	遵守商业道德 促进行业共建	负责任采购 反不正当竞争 推进科技创新 与合作伙伴开展战略合作 组织开展行业交流
社区	加强社区共建 助力公益慈善	开展志愿服务 助力乡村振兴 促进社会就业 倡导文明出行
环境	遵守环境法律法规 保护环境	节能减排 推广新能源车辆 垃圾分类和"光盘行动" 倡导绿色出行 绿色公益

举行《北京公交百年志》首发式

开展"奋进新征程 公交新变化 暨2023年新媒体网络大V
进公交"活动

客七分公司开展安全月宣传活动

以T116路为载体打造"运河文化车厢",树立公交特色线路品牌

焦点·2022

1月

创新产品"优享巴士"业务上线，采用"定线定站，计划性排班，成团后按需派车"的运营模式，实现乘客在线参与拼团预约出行

北京冬奥会北京和延庆赛区各上会团队人员和车辆进驻场站和驻地，1月21日起开始执行运输服务任务，实行闭环管理

2月

集团公司党政联合印发《北京公共交通控股（集团）有限公司"十四五"发展规划和2035年远景目标纲要》

公交技校欧辉客车新能源实训基地落成

发布《北京公共交通控股（集团）有限公司建设产教融合型企业三年规划（2021-2023年）》

3月

完成全国"两会"交通服务保障

完成北京冬奥会、冬残奥会交通服务保障任务，收到北京冬奥组委、挪威奥委会、国家体育总局、延庆区政府以及场馆酒店寄来的感谢信和锦旗80余件次

与丰田公司在北京2022年冬奥会赛区首钢园区合作开展自动驾驶车辆载客运营

8月

印发《北京公交集团构建现代行车安全管理新体系工作方案》

发布"一路同行"数字化公交出行服务APP

有轨电车公司在西郊线设立"暑期开放日"，邀请40余名中小学生走进运营生产一线，了解保障城市运行的轨道交通日常工作情况和有轨电车历史

修订《北京公共交通控股（集团）有限公司劳动合同管理规定》

9月

完成2022年中国国际服务贸易交易会交通服务保障任务

开通定制公交"通学服务"，利用定制公交APP及微信小程序平台，建立与学校、家长的沟通互动机制，征集通学线路出行需求

交通运输部安全与质量监督管理司副司长丁彦昕带领检查组到北京公交检查重大活动保障筹备情况，指导开展安全生产工作

举行2022年驾驶员"金、银方向盘奖"颁奖仪式

调整T105路、317路引入张家湾设计小镇，方便入驻园区乘客出行

10月

与中国邮政集团有限公司北京市分公司签署战略合作协议，共同探索"交邮合作"新机制

举行《北京公交百年志》首发式

集团公司博士后科研工作站首批博士后研究人员进站

完成年度碳排放履约与排放控制责任

积极组织广大党员干部职工，通过电视直播、网络直播、广播等多种媒体平台聆听观看党的二十大开幕盛况，感受团结、奋进的时代脉动

4月

被中共中央、国务院授予"北京冬奥会、冬残奥会突出贡献集体"称号

白洋淀码头及周边道路景观改造提升工程完成项目竣工验收

以色列驻华大使潘绮瑞女士率使团访问北京公交，希望进一步加强科技产业的交流与合作，用科技造福两国人民

5月

与北京微芯区块链与边缘计算研究院签署战略合作协议，推动构筑数字公交新图景，打造公共交通行业数字化转型的"北京样板"

北京北汽出租汽车集团商务分公司贵宾车队执行习近平主席会见香港特别行政区第六任行政长官李家超的交通服务保障任务

配合北京丰台站周边道路开通及北京丰台站临时公交站台建成，新开专149路、调整专4路，为丰台站开通运营提供公交接驳保障

7月

印发实施《北京公交集团关于支持定制公交发展的工作措施》，推动定制公交快速发展

9300余辆公交车助力公益宣传，积极营造社会各界关爱关心新就业者的良好氛围

加强与市、区两级精神文明促进中心的沟通共建，组织各单位开展形式多样、内容丰富的站台文明引导员慰问、座谈交流等活动

为提高乘客满意度及运行效率，亦庄T1线首末三班12组列车行车单程点从49分钟缩短至45分钟

选派高级副职管理人员季欣荣同志作为北京市第十批援藏干部，参加为期3年的对口支援西藏工作

6月

正式承接通州全域70条公交线路，并由所属城市副中心客运有限公司负责通州全域906平方公里区域公交线路的运营工作

向定点帮扶的门头沟区斋堂镇法城村、高铺村和黄岭西村3个集体经济薄弱村捐赠约1万元的防疫物资

市政协党组书记、主席魏小东带队到北京公交开展"一企一组"专题调研

公交车实现刷卡扫码同步查验健康码信息功能

印发实施《北京公交集团深化新时代保修体制机制改革总体方案》

落实中轴线申遗工作要求，110路迁出天桥公交场站

11月

在丽泽商务区推出巡游定制公交服务

高分通过国家级社会管理和公共服务综合标准化试点项目终期评估

在第四届微课大赛全国总决赛中包揽十强，并斩获20项个人单项奖，其中，客八分公司王庆辉登上了金科奖PK赛的舞台

新开502路、调整396路，方便三家店、五里坨等地区乘客通过石广路快速路快速接驳地铁6号线

12月

主导修订的北京市地方标准《公共汽车通用技术条件》（标准号：DB11/T 532-2022）由北京市市场监督管理局批准发布

开通361路、362路、363路、365路和367路5条雄安新区容城县城乡客运线路

印发《北京公交集团品牌线路建设方案》

新开跨区域外围普线903路，成为房山区直达门头沟区的骨干线路，日客运量最高突破10000人次

文旅区西区公交中心站完工，回龙观公交保养场及场站工程实现基本完工，福寿岭公交中心站实现主体结构封顶

公交驿栈便民服务项目第一批11处标的完成合作经营协议签约，首台公交便民移动餐车在崇文门111路公交场站落地运营

国企改革三年行动圆满收官，高质量完成6个方面99项重点改革任务

责任荣誉

北京公交集团、所属单位部分荣誉和奖项

集团公司被中共中央、国务院授予"北京冬奥会、冬残奥会突出贡献集体"称号

集团公司被中国安全生产协会评为"2022年全国安全文化建设示范企业"

集团公司荣获中国节能协会"节能减排科技进步奖"二等奖

集团公司"北京公交数字化运营关键技术应用"案例在中国信息通信研究院与中国通信企业协会联合主办的"2022数字化转型发展高峰论坛"上荣获"鼎新杯"数字化转型应用行业融合应用一等奖

集团公司"同行"文化品牌荣获全国交通运输行业文化品牌"榜样品牌"第一名

集团公司项目荣获第三十六届北京市企业管理现代化创新成果一等奖

集团公司荣获北京市交通安全工作部门联席会颁发的北京市2022年度"市级交通安全优秀系统"称号

集团公司荣获北京市委宣传部授予的"2022年北京市版权保护示范单位"称号

集团公司荣获北京市发改委和生态环境局联合授予的"北京市节能减排先进集体"称号

集团公司"北京公交建企100周年主题曲《百年公交》正式发布"被北京市新闻学会评为北京专业报刊新闻一等奖

集团公司、北汽出租汽车集团有限责任公司荣获北京市冬奥交通保障指挥调度中心授予的"北京2022年冬奥会和冬残奥会交通服务保障企业"称号

北汽出租汽车集团有限责任公司荣获北京市委、市政府授予的"北京冬奥会、冬残奥会北京市先进集体"称号

集团公司、第六客运分公司第十二车队荣获中华全国总工会授予的"2022年全国工会职工书屋示范点"称号

集团公司、第一客运分公司、第二客运分公司、第四客运分公司、第五客运分公司、第六客运分公司、第七客运分公司荣获北京市交通安全工作部门联席会授予的北京市2022年度"市级交通安全先进单位"称号

有轨电车公司荣获中华全国总工会等单位授予的2020-2021年度全国"安康杯"竞赛优胜单位荣誉

电车分公司动物园枢纽站管理中心党总支部"传承公交精神、永葆初心赓续——新'五好'经验做法为基层党建工作赋能蓄力"入选交通运输行业基层党建创新案例企业类十佳案例

第二客运分公司荣获北京市总工会颁发的"2022年首都劳动奖状"

第八客运分公司第三车队877线路荣获北京市总工会授予的"北京市工人先锋号"称号

第三客运分公司男子汉优质服务示范团队荣获北京市交通委员会授予的"平安交通奋斗者·北京榜样"优秀十强集体称号

员工部分荣誉和奖项

第六客运分公司粘志宽荣获全国总工会授予的2022年全国五一劳动奖章、北京团市委评选的2022年"北京青年榜样"年度人物

第五客运分公司崔嫚荣获共青团中央、人力资源和社会保障部授予的第21届"全国青年岗位能手"称号

集团公司宣传部王超在国务院国资委新闻中心和中央企业媒体联盟主办的第九届"国企好新闻"上荣获新闻创客提名奖

集团公司宣传部寇静、徐龙、赵诗雯，电车分公司杨胜荣获北京市新闻学会授予的2021年度北京专业报刊好新闻一等奖

第八客运分公司安全服务部副经理王志荣获北京2022年冬残奥会交通运输服务保障先进个人、北京2022年冬奥会、冬残奥会北京市先进个人、北京市安全生产先进个人、北京市交通委员会"平安交通奋斗者•北京榜样"三十强个人

第一客运分公司695路驾驶员杜建平等7人荣获北京市总工会授予的"首都劳动奖章"

第三客运分公司第十八车队驾驶员孙崎峰荣获北京市国资委授予的2022年度"国企楷模•北京榜样"称号

第七客运分公司第十一车队驾驶员常景生在中共北京市委宣传部、首都文明办主办的2022年"北京榜样"活动中荣获8月份第一周榜样人物

第三客运分公司陈萌、刘然，第五客运分公司樊路彬荣获首都文明委评选的"2022年度首都最美志愿服务家庭"称号

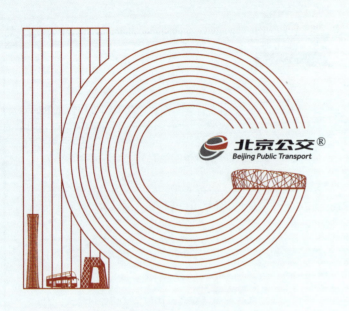

北京公交®
Beijing Public Transport

十年

思变求新，笃行致远

一辆辆流动的公交车，承载着时代的记忆，见证着城市的变迁。这十年，每个晨曦与日暮，都有北京公交的倾情守候；每次重大活动和支援，都有北京公交的严阵以待；每场转型和升级，都有北京公交的焕新前行。历经大战大考，行过万千道路，北京公交于改革中蜕变，蜕变中成长，成长中奋进，初心不改，奋勇前行。行驶在新起点上，北京公交将继续服务四方来客，为新时代首都发展注入澎湃的公交动力，让北京公交这道流动的风景线绽放出更加绚丽的光彩。

响应联合国可持续发展目标

9 产业、创新和基础设施

10 减少不平等

11 可持续城市和社区

十年前行 满载责任

光影流转间,北京公交连续十年披露履责信息。我们胸怀梦想,昂首阔步,用心传达为民理念,精心书写责任故事,满载希望的车上,我们携手更多群体奔赴美好。

数字里的十年

一里一程走过千万,一人一辆汇聚无限。我们用跳动的数字串联出企业发展的蓬勃生机,丈量出首都线网的日新月异,述说着服务民生的殷殷情怀,创造出显著的经济、环境和社会的综合价值。

2013-2022年

累计行驶里程 **121.37** 亿公里
平均每年行驶 **12.14** 亿公里
相当于每年绕地球行驶 **30286** 圈

公共电汽车累计客运量 **317.88** 亿人次
平均每年客运量 **31.79** 亿人次
相当于十年运送全球人口的 **3.97** 倍

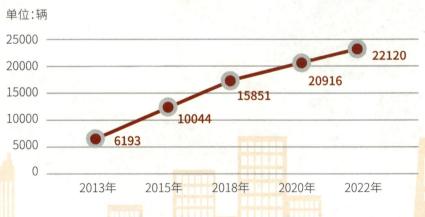

单位:辆

6193　10044　15851　20916　22120

2013年　2015年　2018年　2020年　2022年

清洁能源和新能源公交车总量

合优化报告结构框
，履责实践章节更加
统凝练，加大人物故
、实践故事体量，以丰
的笔触刻画责任内

2021

邀请更多利益相关方参
与报告编制，系统展示
了百年公交技术装备、
运营服务、重大保障、人
才建设等方面的变革和
历史性跨越，设计形式
上更加灵活、丰富，携手
更多伙伴一起向未来。

2022

首次设置两个责任专
题，以"过去—现在—未
来"的结构串联报告内
容，描绘下一个百年的
美好前景，首次以中英
文双语面向全球首播发
布，责任之旅更加系统
完善。

十年履责，初心不改。第
十本报告是总结，更是
新的开始，结构上突出
十年创新变革重点行
动，丰富2022年履责举
措，满载责任继续向前。

线网
线汇成网，连接你我

◎2013年

在全国率先推出定制公交服务模式，受到了乘客好评和社会各界的认可。

◎2019年

通过房山区等地"村村通"公交建设，提升农村改革创新能力，助力北京城乡一体化建设。

◎2020年

承接经济技术开发区区域公交暨亦庄公司启动仪式。

◎2014年

重新构建夜班公交线网。

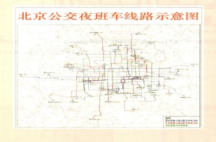

◎2019年

与祥龙资产公司举行祥龙公交移交签约仪式，北京城区公交全面实现一体化运营。

◎2021年

巡游定制公交开通运营，满足望京、环球度假区等6处出行热点区域内乘客短途出行需求。

◎2015年

与房山区人民政府签署战略合作协议，接收房山区凯捷风客运有限公司。

◎2020年

中标雄安高铁站定点班车运营服务项目，雄安新区首个建成区地面公交运营服务项目落地。

◎2022年

正式承接通州区域全部70条公交线路，进一步实现北京地面公交一体化。

场站

更立体现代的枢纽，带来更综合稳定的保障

◎2013年

北京公交首个标准化示范场站吴庄站正式投入运营。

◎2018年

北京市首座现代化公交保养场——王佐公交保养场正式开工建设。

◎2021年

环球影城主题公园配套服务场站——施园公交首末站完工。

◎2016年

北京首个综合公交立体停车楼在马官营公交场站开工建设。

◎2019年

延庆综合交通服务中心（公交停保中心）开工建设。

◎2022年

通州区文旅西区中心站完工。

◎2017年

国内首个停放纯电动公交车的机械式停车楼二通厂公交停车楼开工。

◎2020年

北京首座具有P+R功能的公交立体停车设施——郭公庄公交场站及立体停车楼工程完工。

◎2022年

刘娘府公交首末站开工。

十年变革 发展为民

人民有所呼,改革有所应。一路走来,我们心怀为民初心,锐意进取,开拓创新,始终与党和国家同心同向,与乘客心意相通,为城市交通倾力贡献,以博大的胸襟和开阔的视野求发展、谋突破,持续关注并不断满足人民对美好出行的需要,推动企业向高新技术密集型现代客运出行综合服务商转变。

数字化转型催生发展新动能

数字化转型是全方位、全领域、全流程的综合性系统工程,是培育未来竞争新优势的战略先手棋。进入新时代的十年里,我们主动响应数字交通发展新趋势,依托5G、物联网、人工智能、区块链、云计算、大数据、边缘计算等新兴技术,以数据为核心、网络为连接、平台为驱动,以新基建、新技术、新场景为切入点,推动数字化技术深度融合和广泛应用,带动公交运营产品与服务不断迭代更新,让公交的现代化进程不断加快。

数字化转型与升级,成为促进北京公交高质量发展、提供公共出行高品质服务的重要内容,也让公交出行的价值持续提升和闪耀。

我们逐步夯实数字化的基础,搭建起"数字化云平台"和"数据湖",构建"一个公交云平台、六个业务应用平台、四个保障体系"的数字化总体架构。同时建设和完善运营调度、票务管理、车辆资源、物资管理、人力资源、财务管理、法务管理等75个信息化管理系统,在企业内部注入数字活力,提升各专业工作效率,以数字化驱动变革。

十年数字化变革,是北京公交一路走来的持久追求与暖心回应,满足乘客更好的出行需求是我们始终不渝的使命和担当。

我们将"公交+互联网"的思维和技术手段充分落地应用,建立实时动态出行信息预报系统,开发使用手机APP,提供出行规划、到站提醒、线路查询、乘客拥挤度查询等服务,注册用户超过2600万人次。在运营调度模式转变方面,我们以客流数据为导向,通过信息化建设与运营管理的深度融合,实现了自动计划、智能排班、动态调度,将分散的702处调度单元转化为集成化的41处区域智能调度中心,平均调度车次提高至476次,车次兑现率达到99%以上,发车准点率达到98%以上。

未来,我们将以数字化为引擎,继续探索公交企业数字化升级发展的新方向、新模式、新机制,推动数字化与各专业、各领域相互配合、相互促进、相得益彰。同时推动新型基础设施赋能传统基础设施升级改造,实现传统公交向数字公交转型,引领公交行业创新可持续发展。

北京公交运营调度指挥中心

第一客运分公司芍药居区域智能调度中心

电车分公司南坞区域智能调度中心

快速直达专线

合乘定制公交

定制商务班车

巡游定制公交

多样化公交更懂您

北京公交致力于让更多的人享受更好的公共出行服务，引领公众出行方式，提升城市生活品质。我们创新多样化公交的特色服务，推出多种产品，用最真诚的行动践行着"以乘客为中心"的初心使命，继承和发扬着北京公交百年文化、百年情怀、百年传统，不断深化客运出行服务内涵、拓展城市客运出行空间，交出满足乘客多样化、差异化、高品质的出行需求的公交答案。

北京公交首开全国多样化公交服务先河，在全国首推定制公交，每一条线路的开通都体现了"量体裁衣、按需而设"的服务理念。

2011年4月，我们联合昌平区交通局，在天通苑、回龙观两大社区网推出了预定专座的社区通勤快车服务，这是我们对多样化公交最初的思考和探索，也为定制公交的推出积累了宝贵的经验。

2013年8月，为保证定制商务班车顺利开通，我们组织了近百人的专业队伍，分组对100多个小区、写字楼进行踏勘，对小区规模、位置、道路通行条件、停站待客地点、最佳运营线路等深入了解。北到昌平，南到大兴，西到房山，东到燕郊，线路踏勘人员把预计乘客集中的点位一个不落地踏勘了一遍。同时，幕后负责定制班车平台开发和信息化服务的北京公交人，在网上平台成功上线之前披星戴月、日夜奋战。2013年9月9日，全国首条定制商务班车在京通快速路开通运营，多样化公交出行自此走进北京公交运营，成为北京公交便利市民个性化出行、助力交通拥堵治理和引领绿色出行的一项创新服务举措。

多样化公交"家族成员"的不断扩大，推动了公交服务向高品质升级，践行"出行即生活"，实现广大乘客的出行从"挤公交"到"坐公交"再到"享公交"的蜕变。

随后，快速直达专线、节假日专线、高铁快巴、休闲旅游专线、合乘定制公交、儿研所专线、需求响应式公交等多样化服务陆续推出。同时，定制公交APP、网站、微信、小程序等端口全部投入使用，乘客可以随时高效预约出行，大幅提升了乘客的定制体验。我们在最大限度发挥公共交通的集约化优势、改善地面公交服务水平和满足居民多层次出行需求的同时，全面提升了乘客在城市发展中的获得感。

经常乘坐巡游定制公交的高先生谈到："我目前上班是先通过巡游定制公交到地铁站，中间主要以乘坐地铁为主，出来到公司就不用坐车，走两步就到了。所以说巡游定制公交就是相当于我从小区到地铁站的主要交通方式，由于它的便捷舒适，早晚高峰都能覆盖，所以我几乎每天都会乘坐。"

人享其行，未来可期。

面对城市出行发展新趋势，我们将更好地激活供给、引导需求，持续创新服务模式、丰富服务产品，提高多样化出行服务与人们美好需求的匹配度，精心打造多样化出行方式，不断提升人民群众的获得感和幸福感，实现首都公交高质量发展、高品质服务和高效能治理。

无障碍出行不再遥远

无障碍出行是国家和社会文明的标志,其建设水平事关人民群众获得感、幸福感、安全感,事关交通强国建设质量,事关亿万家庭福祉。北京公交致力于为每一位社会成员搭建连接外界的桥梁,让出行不便的人群走出家门、参与社会生活、展示自我价值,从无障碍"硬设施"的改良完善,到"软服务"的优化供给,不断破解着无障碍出行的现实命题。

时代推进融合无障碍,社会呼唤交通无障碍,大众需要畅行无障碍,北京公交为满足城市发展与人们出行需求,与时俱进完善无障碍建设,优化无障碍服务。

随着人口老龄化程度的进一步加深,民众对出行无碍性、包容性、安全性的要求越来越高。截至2022年底,北京市60岁及以上人口达到465.1万人,公共交通已成为更多老年人青睐的出行方式。建设覆盖面广、安全性高和连接顺畅的无障碍出行服务,打造面向所有群体的包容性公共交通体系,是我们优化无障碍出行环境的出发点和落脚点。

"双奥"的举办,是我们深度融入无障碍服务的阶段,尤其在2019年,北京市启动全市无障碍环境建设专项行动,我们以此为契机,广泛开展无障碍服务提升活动,进一步提升无障碍服务的意识和能力,圆满完成了2022年冬奥会、冬残奥会期间的公交无障碍服务保障工作。自此,我们在无障碍出行方面积累了丰富的"双奥"遗产。

我们用心用情做好每一个细节,让化"碍"为"爱"不再是一句口号,而是让其成为北京公交对特殊群体的共识和承诺。

硬件设施建设与完善是无障碍服务的第一步。我们加大购置无障碍车辆、改造升级站台的投入力度,优化既有运营线路设计,灵活调整运营力量,完善站台车厢联动式无障碍服务模式,打造无障碍服务精品示范线。同时,细致完善扶手、地锚、

无障碍导板公交车方便使用轮椅的老年人乘车

帮助老年人乘坐低地板公交车

无障碍导板公交车方便使用轮椅的残疾人乘车

在公交车上帮助残疾人固定轮椅

公交车入站停靠距站台50厘米方便无障碍出行

无障碍踏板等设施，并研发无障碍导乘系统，进一步方便老年乘客、残障乘客的使用。目前，我们配备低地板车辆1.4万余辆，其中带无障碍导板车辆1.2万余辆，城区无障碍公交车占比超过80%，6条线路被推荐为北京市无障碍服务精品示范线路。同时，通过与市交通委、市残联、市老龄办等部门加强沟通交流，反复研判优化无障碍服务设计，积极开展常态化教育与专项整治活动，以车轮距站台50厘米为标准，不断提高驾驶员靠边停车，停直对正的驾驶技能，以一次次躬身体验和反复训练，切身感知老年人等群体的不便，并通过运营大数据排查老年群体等乘客乘车集中的线路和时间，建立无障碍重点线站"档案"，更有针对性地提高服务水平。

无障碍出行不仅需要连接外界，更需要连接情感。我们在解决完善无障碍设施"有没有"的同时，着眼于无障碍服务"好不好""优不优"的问题。

我们积极落实市委市政府关于敬老助残、无障碍环境建设的指示精神，构建了无障碍服务保障管理体系，建立了集团班子挂钩、分公司班子督点、车队班子包站的千人包千站无障碍服务管理新模式。同时，组织开展"敬老助残"活动，加强广泛宣传，在全系统、全社会营造浓厚的敬老助残服务氛围，不断提升老年乘客、残障乘客的乘车体验，用恰到好处的关爱，让无障碍出行更加自然、更有尊严。

我们将一直用面向未来的包容和不断进步的细节温暖每个人的出行之路。

创造一个全龄友好的无障碍出行环境，使每个社会成员都受益，是全社会的共同责任，也是北京公交作为首都地面公交运营主体的担当。未来，我们将传承"双奥"无障碍建设遗产，秉承中华优秀传统文化理念，创新融入先进技艺与设备，为老年乘客、残障乘客打造无障碍出行环境，助力首都城市建设全龄无障碍出行首善之区，引领全国无障碍出行建设。

市交通委政务服务中心调研北京公交
"接诉即办"工作

公交集团五月份"接诉即办"
工作讲评会

基层人员上站台服务

"接诉即办"管理中心工作间

听民声 解民忧

"我就住新北社区，以前出门想坐508路，往南往北都得走好几百米，现在一出门就能坐上了，真是方便多了，为北京公交集团的工作效率点赞！"市民刘大爷说。这是在居民通过"接诉即办"反映出行总"绕远"，对北京公交增设站点之后的认可，这份认可对我们"接诉即办"工作人员来说弥足珍贵，"民之所呼 我有所应"是我们的满腔热忱，也是持久服务的动力源泉。

在新时代创新城市治理的深刻变革中，一根热线"绣花针"，穿起民生"万根线"。北京公交作为承担北京地面公交主体任务、保障民生的公共服务类企业，在2019年专门成立了"接诉即办"管理中心，更好地服务乘客，满足乘客诉求，提高乘客满意度。

乘客的一趟趟出行关乎千家万户的生活，承载或大或小的梦想，也汇聚了一代又一代的城市记忆，所以我们重视乘客的每一件诉求，紧盯每一件"关键小事"。

我们始终以乘客需求为导向，以乘客诉求为哨声，通过有效方式和途径主动为乘客办实事、解难题，努力搭建起公交和乘客之间的信任关系和沟通桥梁。我们实行7x24小时签办，建立了日常派单"当天核实安抚、三天给予答复、五天办结上报"的快速响应机制。为核实一个诉求，多个部门协同会商，只为乘客反映的问题能够及时反馈，确保实现"件件有答复、事事有回音"。

对待乘客的诉求，行动就是最大的诚意。

我们会认真核对每一件诉求，精准定性，精准派单，将"接诉即办"的数据分析融入线路布局优化、编制时刻表等工作中，开展公交线网评价、优化辅助决策支持、线网优化跟踪评价工作，增强线网优化工作的公信力。把乘客诉求多的线路、时段作为工作的着力点，明确各层级人员工作职责和线路开调延业务流程，做实、做细线路开调延工作，努力提升服务质量。

案例

用心倾听，用脚踏勘，只为方便人们的出行

2022年，西六环附近的杨坨、三家店地区随着基础设施的完善和大量人口的入住，换乘需求不断增大，我们在接到市民的诉求后起，多次进行实地勘察，走访重点站位的乘客，并且在附近小区征集居民意见，细致了解民众对线路具体走向、站位设置、发车时间等实际需求，设计了一条由杨坨开往金安桥东，连接门头沟区和石景山区的新线路。经过2个多月的共同奋战，完成了行车计划制定、车辆标识张贴、站杆站牌设置等工作，502路的正式开通，实现了门头沟区杨坨、军庄、三家店等区域连接石景山区的快速出行，通勤时间得以缩短，方便乘客公共出行。

我们进一步推动向"主动治理、未诉先办、一办到底"转变，通过深度分析准确掌握民意风向标。

我们通过"日、周、月、季"情况通报制度全面感知民意，为提升服务精准"画像"：比如乘客反映排名前十的问题是什么、变化趋势怎么样、相关部门和单位承办的事项进展如何……希望通过一个问题的解决，带动一类问题的解决。此外，我们定期研判分析乘客意见的种类和趋势，有针对性地开展专项治理，做到发生投诉讲评案例，未发生投诉研判风险点，希望通过向前一步的预判和未雨绸缪，让乘客的幸福感、获得感和安全感不断提升。2022年，诉求解决率99.14%，环比提高4.83%，满意率99.11%，环比提高3.41%，逐步实现更好更快地响应。

"接诉即办"工作只有进行时，没有完成时。

2023年，"接诉即办"改革即将走过第4年，在这期间，一条服务热线连接四方乘客，北京公交与乘客的距离越来越近，同时也收获了乘客的理解、支持、信赖与期待。未来，我们将始终倾听，让声声民意得到回应，在持续梳理经验中增益实践，同时进一步引导市民主动参与地面公交治理，推动更多人共建共治共享。

专家寄语：立足新起点，开启新未来

全国政协委员、交通运输部科学研究院

副院长兼总工程师 王先进

公共交通是一座城市重要的基础设施，是一项关系民生的社会公益事业，也是城市文明进步的重要标志。

经过百年发展，北京公交提供的公共出行服务基本做到了地域广覆盖、人群均等化、城乡一体化，为首都公共交通高质量发展作出了巨大贡献。交通运输部科学研究院与北京公交开展过多项合作，既是北京公交发展、建设的参与者与实践者，也是北京公交发展路上的见证者与受益者。近几年，城市公共交通领域快速发展，乘客需求越来越多元化，车辆设备越来越绿色智能，对公交运营企业提出了更高的要求。

为缓解交通拥堵、出行不便和环境污染等矛盾，我国日益重视"城市优先发展公共交通"战略。近年来，《交通强国建设纲要》《国家综合立体交通网规划纲要》等文件为深入实施公交优先发展战略指明方向。

北京公交置身于这样的外部环境，需要深刻理解公交优先发展背后不同利益相关方的期望和诉求。对于政府部门，公交优先就是把公交发展放在城市建设发展的优先位置，优先配置公交优先发展所需要的资源，包括交通通道，客运场站等空间和土地资源。对于公众，公交优先意味着给予公交优先级物权，包括使用频次较高的校车、班车都应该得到优先使用；同时，也意味着公交具备良好合理的可承担可支付能力。只有做到"供需精准对接"，北京公交才能更有针对性地推动各方落实公交优先发展战略。

王先进带队到北京公交开展跨党派调研联学活动

数字化、智能化的浪潮席卷之下，数字化转型已成为公共交通行业促进新旧动能转换、转型升级的战略抉择和必由之路。

北京公交近年来一直在运用智能调度提升公交速度，利用大数据对公交线路公交网络进行客流分析，既进一步满足了公众乘用公交的需求，也提升了政府资源配置的效率，这也正是数字化转型所追求的价值目标。从总体来看，北京公交在数字化转型方面仍有一定的提升空间，可从以下五个方面进一步发展完善：一是要夯实数字化基础，补齐基础设施和基础资源；二是要抓住数据应用的牵引，做好数据中心建设；三是把握数据流动的要求，打破数据孤岛，真正实现数据共享；四是培育交通数据市场；五是要强化数据安全的保障。基于此，才能建立对数字化转型全面系统的认知和判断，乘势而上，跨出数字化发展的新高度。

- -

行业发展，人才先行。交通运输部对整个交通运输行业人才发展战略和人才资源开发政策十分重视。

加快建设总量充足、结构优化、布局合理、素质优良的人才队伍是总体目标，其中城市公交、智慧交通、综合交通发展等交通运输急需紧缺人才也是重点培养的方向。2020年，北京公交设立全国首个公交行业博士后科研工作站，这是首创性的举措，对于行业发展至关重要。北京公交依托其丰富的应用场景，为人才成长提供了良好的研究场域，希望北京公交将人才的全方位培养抓得更实更细，把全方位做好人才的引进、培养和使用放在更加优先的位置，让公交行业既能够事业留人、感情留人，还有合理的收入待遇留人，加速创新成果向现实生产力转化，使博士后人才在赋能传统公交转型升级和高质量发展中发挥更大的支持作用。

2022年恰逢北京公交发布社会责任报告十周年，这是一个全新的起点，希望北京公交能够再接再厉，面对新的挑战继续开拓创新，构建一个更人本、更健康、更安全、更绿色、更可持续的公共交通新网络。

服务
民之所需, 行之所至

细致入微为乘客, 是北京公交道不尽的世纪传承, 亦是公交人诉不完的满腔深情。我们锚定"为民坐标", 于大局主动创新引领发展, 于细节用心用情至臻完善, 在周而复始的晨昏交割中, 为生活拓展行进空间, 为城市延伸无限可能, 传递每一个或大或小的梦想, 生动诠释着人民的出行有始发站与终点站, 北京公交服务无止境。

密织线网畅通城市脉动

面对客运服务市场"提质降本增效"新要求,我们进一步完善"干、普、微"三级公交线网布局,开展准点工程,积极配合落实回大地区、城市副中心重点工程和轨道接驳,灵活调整设站和运营时间,推进公交与首都城市功能的协同衔接,提高公交通达性、准点率,将线路优化做到乘客心坎里。

539 条线路
实现准点工程

公交准点发车率
98.83%

"减加结合"优化线网布局

- 全年开调延线路100条,其中新开线路12条、调整线路78条、撤销线路10条
- 增加线网覆盖82.5公里,方便118个小区居民出行
- 削减重复线路长度276公里、减少重复设站700处

做好轨道接驳工作

- 推进地铁16号线榆树庄公交站台设置,在678路导改路由上设站,实现就近接驳轨道站点
- 研提昌平线南延学院桥等公交加站道路设施改造需求,配合地铁新线开通,实现公交加站
- 结合地铁东管头南站临时站台的修建,调整49路、845路接驳地铁
- 对全市361个轨道站点的1023个出入口逐个摸排调查。按照"一站一策"的原则,提升30米接驳距离的轨道站点比例

深入推进准点工程

- 通过推出定点发车线路、强化时刻表管理等措施,提升运营效能
- 试点开展中途区段准点工作,在210条线路上实现调度员利用智能调度系统监控车辆中途准点情况

2020—2022年运营指标统计表

	指标	2020年	2021年	2022年
运营线路	运营线路总数（条）	1214	1225	1299
	常规公交线路条数（条）	1207	1217	1291
	常规公交线路长度（公里）	28418.4	28579.7	30173.9
	线网长度（公里）	7628.6	7771.3	8180.6
	站位数（个）	18834	19262	20469
优化线网	优化线路总数（条）	212	151	100
	减少重复线路长度（公里）	470.7	384.6	276.0
	削减重复设站（个）	1083	941	700
	解决有路无车里程(公里)	167.8	142.7	82.5
	方便小区出行（个）	440	186	118

更多出行选择

我们基于乘客的不同出行需求，创新公交发展模式，形成了以定制公交为主，集合区域巡游、通学线路、旅游观光、就医专线、深山摆渡、定制快巴等特色服务线路，在提供多样化、差异化、品质化的公共出行服务的同时，让每一条特色定制公交线路也成为城市流动的风景线。截至2022年底，我们的巡游定制公交业务已在望京、环球度假区、苏家坨、旧宫、丰台科技园、回龙观地区、永丰、朱辛庄、亦庄、天通苑、西二旗、沙河、稻香湖、南锣鼓巷、北神树、丽泽商务区16个区位开通。

开进丽泽商务区的巡游定制公交

定制公交累计开行线路

418条（区位）

多样化公交专线达

158条

"地面公交是城市出行中重要的组成部分，未来，应面向全过程、全链条出行服务，加快形成全覆盖的公交路权，确保公交速度和可靠性，提升吸引力和竞争力，同时探索大规模、可预约的公交出行服务。"

——北京交通发展研究院院长 郭继孚

公交先行赋能一体化发展

交通一体化是京津冀协同发展的骨干系统和先行区域。我们紧跟京津冀交通协同政策，积极融入京津冀城市群建设，在公共交通出行方面做了许多探索。我们不断扩大公交客运版图，大力实施"城优郊进"，承接通州区域公交线路，进一步实现北京地面公交一体化。全力支持雄安新区公共交通规划建设，扩大容城组团项目线路规模，提升雄县组团公共交通服务水平，助力雄安新区打造集绿色水域、特色旅游、生态产业为一体的智慧交通示范区，推动京津冀一体化发展从蓝图迈向现实。

已获得雄安新区线路特许经营权

19条

开通雄安新区定制公交

3条

线路总长度

347.1公里

所辖运营车辆

146辆

雄安容城组团303路开通运营

正式承接，"通"字头线路全面焕新

倾听故事

> 我们持续推进'两网'纵深融合发展，让轨道、公交一体化换乘更顺畅、更舒适，不断推动公共交通互联互通，通过'共建、联建'打造'服务共同体'，充分发挥北京公交助力京津冀一体化发展的先行作用。

北京市通州区交通局副局长
林青

2022年，北京公交承接通州区域的全部公交线路，为加快构建快速、便捷、高效的互联互通综合交通网络、纵深推进京津冀一体化发展提供了坚实基础和有力保障。

从2021年2月开始，通州区政府和北京公交成立了专项工作组，双方对整个通州公交的运营现状、场站布局、企业经营状况和改革后的发展方向进行了调查和研究，并建立了周对接机制，在一年半的时间里，双方累计召开磋商会100余次，并围绕"人、车、站、线"等重点问题逐个突破。

2022年6月1日，北京公交正式承接通州区域全部70条公交线路，并负责通州全域906平方公里区域公交线路运营，从车型、能源结构到公交站杆站牌、候车亭，通州区域地面公交翻开了崭新的一页，也进一步实现了北京地面公交一体化，为形成"一张图""一张网""一个标准""一套体系"

的首都公交发展新格局打下坚实基础。

当副中心公交在6月1日一夜"换装"，乘客对整个线路的新运营模式一时无法适应，北京公交各级领导高度重视，在重点站台调研问需，及时解决乘客的出行诉求与疑问，让广大乘客拥有良好的乘车体验。

京津冀交通一体化的目的就是要惠及广大的人民，让大家出行、工作和生活更加便利、更加畅通。北京公交承接通州区域公交线路以来，既增强了整个副中心的城市功能，包括统筹城乡发展，也在促进交通一体化方面起到了至关重要的作用。通州区域的公交也变得更加便捷、更加靓丽、更加安全、更具有吸引力。

北京公交正式承接通州全域公交线路后，同步升级运营服务效能，调集新能源公交车辆，并以科技赋能确保行车安全和管理，整个通州区的线网布局更加科学、公交运营更加顺畅。同时，我们将通州悠久的文化底蕴和百年公交浓厚的企业文化有机融合，在多条线路量身打造了具有通州区域特色的车厢文化，营造出独属于北京城市副中心的车厢文化环境，为广大通州市民带来了全新升级的公共出行服务体验。

提升运营服务水平

按照"一线一策"方式，提升45条线路的运营服务水平，不同程度调整线路运营时间和间隔时间，进一步完善公交线网布局

车辆装备焕然一新

调集565辆新能源公交车，积极优化车辆能源结构，实现融合后通州区域公交新能源车辆100%使用，车辆装备舒适性、环保性和安全性大幅提升

设施有效升级改造

制定场站标准化改造和候车亭更新方案，加快公交站务设施的升级改造，充分利用电子站牌、智能手机应用等载体，为乘客提供实时准确的发车时间、到站时间、拥挤度、车辆位置等信息

实现区域智能调度

正式启用城市副中心区域智能调度中心，不断完善通州区域公交智能调度信息化建设，并依托新建的施园场站区域智能调度中心，实现区域化智能调度

正式承接通州区域地面公交

通州区域焕然一新的新能源车辆

具有通州区域特色的车厢文化

位于通州区施园场站的区域智能调度中心

数字转型 智慧出行

我们注重培育数字经济与运营管理的深度融合,持续在智慧公交、数字公交领域着力、聚力、发力,推进系列数字化成果深度落地并广泛应用,升级转变调度模式,实现站杆站牌信息化,丰富人们出行场景,让乘客在数字化场景中悦然畅行。

- 先后发布"智能公交"2.0、3.0系列数字化应用能力包

- 以"数据湖"为支撑,深入开展"机器迭代"学习,推进智能升级,提升调度系统的数字化水平,逐步形成"简化层级、权责清晰、智慧高效"的区域调度体系

- 高效完成车载刷卡机具升级,快速建成健康状态查验平台

- 开发站杆二维码信息生成与查询系统

- 完成数字人民币应用场景和多个支付渠道的技术接入

- 智慧加燃系统、车辆CAN数据应用监控与分析系统上线运行

完成

1815根

电子站牌通电上线服务

案例 开学首日,智能调度保出行

2022年9月1日,北京迎来中小学校开学。中小学开学后,早晚高峰时段接送学生的家长和学生明显增加。为此,北京公交41处区域智能调度中心利用信息化系统,加强远程调度,对道路拥堵、车辆满载、行车间隔等进行实时监控,在240余处场站安排备车600余辆,根据道路拥堵及线路运营情况,及时加入线路运营,减少乘客候车时间,确保运力充足、秩序平稳。

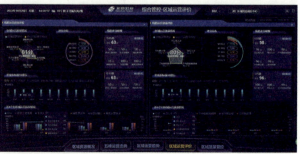

北京公交运营服务数字化管理界面

每一站，与平安相伴

城市的幸福宜居，出行安全是重要前提之一。"人民至上、生命至上"，北京公交以此为念，不畏酷暑严寒，不惧风霜雨雪，一如既往守住安全底线，从细节出发，从微小着手，落实安全责任，消除安全隐患，让满载希望的公交平稳行驶，让乘客与安全同行、与平安相伴。

车行万里 安全第一

安全出行，起于本心，落于微末。我们将行车安全落实、渗透到每一项工作、每一个日常行为中，努力将行车安全隐患风险降到最低，为每位乘客的安全出行、可靠出行保驾护航。

2022年，北京公交制定印发《北京公交集团构建现代行车安全管理新体系工作方案》，持续推进行车安全管理体制机制建设，增强风险防范管控能力，加快智慧安全系统应用，全面提升行车安全管理现代化水平。

累计安装主动安全预警系统的车辆近

8000辆

安装异常行为识别系统的车辆达到

5750辆

累计为重点高速线路、夜班线路、城市副中心线路配发驾驶员多体征情绪感知设备

2150台

持续关注驾驶员身体情况，督促驾驶员按规定及时完成体检；完善驾驶员心理档案，组织开展驾驶员心理适宜性普测

开发驾驶员生物节律管理应用系统，建立驾驶员安全预警模型、精神压力感知模型

保障行车安全举措

开通夜班车实时语音通话系统，为重点高速线路、夜班线路、城市副中心线路驾驶员配发多体征情绪感知设备

试验推广A柱盲区透视预警系统，应用科技手段减少车辆盲区带来的不利影响

"一键报警"装置自查2.15万辆次，保障重点线路"一键报警"系统的全覆盖、无故障

夜间行车安全检查

驾驶员岗前宣誓

夏季防疲劳叮嘱

雪天安全叮嘱

案例 **北京公交为驾驶员配备情绪感知手环**

2022年6月,北京公交正式承接通州区域地面公交,为进一步确保乘客、驾驶员安全,北京公交为通州区域全体驾驶员配发情绪感知手环,对驾驶员的身心异常情况提前预警。情绪感知手环可以实时监测驾驶员的体温、心率、呼吸频率、血氧、运动、血压、睡眠7种体征,还可以监测抑郁、焦虑等情绪状态,为驾驶员心理健康提供坚实保障。如发现驾驶员在发车前或行车途中身体监测数值发生较大波动,车队会安排人员了解驾驶员身体健康状态,叮嘱驾驶员及时就医服药,保证健康作息。必要时,采取换班或暂停驾驶措施,为通州区市民提供安全、放心的乘车环境。

佩戴多体征情绪感知设备的驾驶员

多一份保障 多一份安心

患生于所忽，祸起于细微。我们树立红线意识、坚守底线思维，以安全管理体系完善为导向，着力提升应急管理能力，深化隐患排查治理，全面加强人员安全管理素质支撑，全力筑牢公交的安全堤坝，全心守护千家万户的幸福安康。

○ 稳固安全基础

- 以完善体制"筑安"、提升能力"保安"、聚焦重点"促安"、强化科技"创安"、深入联动"护安"为重点工作，构建现代行车安全管理新体系
- 修订完善《公交停车场站治安消防安全管理规定》等安全管理制度
- 2022年7月集团公司通过安全生产标准化一级达标

○ 隐患排查治理

- 制定集团公司安全生产检查工作制度，规范安全生产检查工作操作标准
- 巩固提升安全生产检查信息化应用，应用隐患排查管理信息系统进行安全生产检查记录
- 推进燃气安全排查整治、房屋安全专项整治、安全专项整顿等工作，及时消除各类隐患
- 持续推进安全生产专项整治三年行动

○ 提升应急管理

- 做好新修订应急预案的宣贯落实，强化全员安全应急培训，拓展应急处置演练，不断提升预警响应能力
- 统筹做好汛期、雪天等特殊天气应急值守和响应工作
- 规范应急值守人员安全应急检查工作，提升企业安全生产管理水平

妥善处置运营车辆上的各类突发事件
3413起

涉及人员
3776人次

开展各类应急演练
6095次

参与人数
84899人次

修订二级单位突发事件应急预案
438个

2020—2022年人防、物防、技防统计表

	项 目	2020年	2021年	2022年
人防	乘务管理员（名）	39069	36679	31630
物防	封闭电子围栏（处）	500	500	500
技防	一键报警系统（辆）	17530	17271	21500
	自动识别系统（套）	15600	17249	24043

安全文化植根于心

我们以"生命至上,安全第一"的思想理念为指引,组织开展多项特色鲜明的安全文化专题活动,通过安全专题培训,安全宣传活动等方式,让"安全成为习惯"印刻在员工心中,让安全文化真正落地生根。

安全教育培训

我们持续推进安全教育培训,为司乘人员、安全管理人员组织专业培训,定期组织相关专题安全培训;通过制作发布《城市公交运营安全警示案例集》、开展行车安全教育课件评比活动、"金、银方向盘奖"表彰、班前宣誓、安全诵读、笔记批阅等宣传教育活动,创新丰富安全教育载体,让"首都无小事、公交无小事"的安全意识入脑入心。

安全主题活动

我们积极开展礼让斑马线、"全国交通安全日"宣传、安全生产月等形式多样的主题活动,营造浓厚的安全文化氛围,潜移默化地提升员工和公众的安全意识。

《城市公交运营安全警示案例集》发布仪式

2022年"金、银方向盘"颁奖仪式

安全教育培训
24.8万人次

获得安全行车最高荣誉
"金方向盘"奖的驾驶员
200名

获得"银方向盘"奖的驾驶员
1232名

在安全生产宣传咨询日、消防大演练等活动中共设置宣传站
305处

发放知识手册
43768册

《城市公交运营安全警示案例集》荣获中国公路学会2022年度全国公路优秀科普作品视频类一等奖

安全宣传咨询日活动

案例 北京公交开展"全国交通安全日"宣传活动

2022年12月2日，北京公交以"文明守法 平安回家"为主题，在全系统开展了第十一个"全国交通安全日"主题宣传教育活动。各客运分公司主动协调并积极配合辖区交管部门，通过日叮嘱、致驾驶员一封信、行车安全知识答卷等多种形式，叮嘱教育在岗驾驶员严格遵守交通安全法律法规、礼让斑马线、文明行车，同时也积极引导广大市民以文明出行为荣，共同维护安全、和谐、有序的交通出行环境，努力营造良好的安全行车氛围。

"全国交通安全日"宣传活动

织牢网络安全防护网

在云计算、大数据、物联网等新型信息技术加速发展的背景下，公交系统的网络规模正逐渐扩大，自主可控始终是实现网络安全的前提条件。我们从网络安全机制入手，打牢网络安全基地，运用技术手段全面监测网络安全漏洞，构筑良好的网络安全意识，促进公交网络安全从意识到防御治理能力全方位提升，保持网络安全平稳可控的向好局势。

持续完善网络安全体系
修订、编制《北京公交集团账号管理制度》《北京公交集团数据安全管理制度》等制度，进一步规范和指导网络安全管理工作

不断增强网络安全意识
开展数据安全和个人信息保护政策及形势、常见网络安全问题分析处理及应急响应措施等主题的宣传与培训工作

及时监测网络安全态势
在核心交换节点处安装部署网络安全态势监测平台，对流量日志进行集中存储、统一分析，集中展示网络安全态势情况

网络安全保障措施

案例　北京公交开展全员软件正版化培训

2022年11月，北京公交开展全员软件正版化培训，教会员工如何识别盗版软件，讲清危害，说明利弊，规范使用，从而加强知识产权保护、保障信息安全的意识。目前，北京公交各平台系统软件全面正版化，保障集团公司各业务系统安全运行，确保公交智慧调度平台、车载票款设备和信息服务设施的平稳运行和信息安全。

软件正版化培训

让你我乐享其"乘"

公交线路有始终，热情服务无终点。作为窗口服务型企业，我们多措并举落实"接诉即办"，创新升级服务方式，用温馨的车厢环境和贴心的关怀问候为乘客营造舒适的乘车环境，提供高质量的窗口服务，让人们爱上公交、享受出行。

持续深化"接诉即办"

知民意方能解民忧。我们认真倾听群众的每一次呼声，用心解决每一个诉求，深化"接诉即办"改革创新，加强机制管理，落实定期汇报、定期通报和预警通报、优化考核激励等制度建设，推动"接诉即办"管理标准化、流程化、制度化，全面提升各专业、各单位诉求办理的意识和能力。同时，持续开展"接诉即办""每月一题"活动，主动开展综合治理，稳步向"未诉先办"迈进。

接线员解答乘客疑问

乘客满意率

93.52%

"接诉即办"诉求同比减少

13377件

下降

21.95%

客户沟通（热线、信箱、现场接待等）

199577次

解决重点、难点、热点问题累计上门

661次

"接诉即办""三率"综合得分

99.24分

畅通渠道真诚问需

为更好地服务乘客，我们多途径畅通与乘客的沟通渠道，聆听乘客声音，了解民生诉求，确保全时响应，真诚做到回复有温度、办理有速度，用专业与温情，回应每一次出行路上的萍水相逢。

 坚持每月上站台、进社区、走车厢，广泛开展座谈交流活动，充分调查了解民意

 提升12345、96166等热线接听办理水平，及时了解乘客需求与意见

 扩大新媒体平台矩阵，充分发挥并利用官网、微信、微博、抖音等平台的优势，加强与乘客的双向互动

 主动策划"粉丝见面会""公交出行达人"等相关活动，加强与乘客的交流，密切与乘客的联系

精品服务只为您满意

我们升级服务举措，深度挖掘推动品牌线路建设，精心打造车厢文化2.0版本，让公交车成为品味城市文化、见证文明城市底色的缩影。同时常态化开展车辆日常清洁、特殊群体服务等，满足乘客多元化、高品质、交互式的美好出行需求。

 案例　**"三迎一创促提升"，全心全意升级服务品质**

为构建与人民群众对美好出行新期待相呼应、与"以乘客为中心"发展理念相适应的现代公交发展面貌，北京公交积极推进"三迎一创促提升"工程，通过落实服务品质提升工程等"八项提升工程"重点任务，服务品质实现新升级，运营发展取得新突破。北京公交先后制定多项服务管理规定，通过专题调研、专项治理、劳动竞赛等活动，进一步增强员工服务意识，并积极打造需求响应公交新样板、大客流品牌线路和无障碍服务精品示范线路，不断提升服务乘客出行品质。

案例　**T116路"运河文化车厢"尽享出行新体验**

第五客运分公司联合通州区委宣传部，以T116路为载体，先后打造了3辆"运河文化车厢"，为游客假期郊游踏青和体验打卡提供了一个新选择。车厢以京杭大运河文化理念为中心，围绕城市副中心旅游景点、运河历史文化、绿色发展理念等重点，以图文展示、云视听介绍、扫码观景、动态灯光等多种方式呈现，让游客的路途变得丰富有趣，获得良好的乘车体验。

"坐着公交车穿梭于城市绿心公园，行驶在大运河畔，欣赏着缤纷运河的美景，回味着'通州八景'带来的历史韵味，这种感觉太好了。"

——家住通州区的乘客李先生

组织人员
5.6万余人次

清洁车辆
13.6万车次

更换标志
1.2万余张

帮扶老年、残障乘客安全乘车
5.2万余人次

布置车厢文化的线路
54条

车辆
2080辆

评选出优质服务示范线路
28条

优质服务示范车组
300个

全力推动品牌线路建设，制定《北京公交品牌线路建设方案》，构建多样化车厢文化新体系，增加扫码服务，提供立体化视觉感受，提升乘车体验

深入聚焦老年人等特殊群体的实际特点，做好日常服务与应急预案工作，多措并举提升无障碍水平，努力提升服务温度

强化服务意识，加强对服务"零容忍""忌语禁行"以及管理人员回复乘客诉求的管理，共计发放"委屈奖"6人次

提升车辆清洁专业化，每月20日组织各单位集中开展车辆卫生清洁日活动，努力为乘客营造干净整洁的乘车环境

案例 **"1路"焕新，首创"公交+云游"出行方式**

2022年10月13日，中国移动北京公司与北京公交联合开展服务创新品牌赋能活动，在1路公交车上推出智慧公交小程序"云游1路"，打造全新"公交+文旅"车厢文化，共同为广大市民乘客提供更加多样的出行服务体验。"云游1路"小程序设置地图导览、走进1路、云游VR三个板块，乘客可以通过观看手绘风导览地图、聆听实时讲解、深度了解沿途重要建筑和景点，还可以通过长按二维码"隔空"体验"中国红"的时代感，为乘客带来虚拟现实结合、线上线下一体的全新"大1路"乘车体验。

『云游1路』小程序界面

站台敬老助残

敬老车厢文化

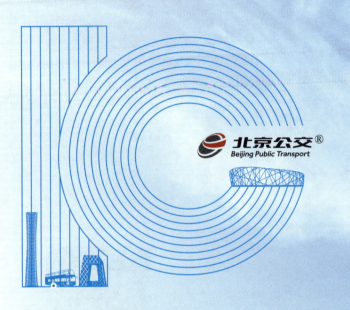

担当
方向盘上,用心坚守

北京公交作为首都地面公交运行主体,始终与党和国家同心同向,为社会分忧解难,在历次国家政治任务和重大盛典活动的服务任务中勇挑重担。北京公交人一次又一次用热情真诚、优质周到的交通服务保障,在历次"大考"中不断擦亮底色,向首都市民、向世界展现出了大国公交风采。

冰雪映照下的冬奥保障

北京冬奥会以立春之日的"一片雪花"拉开了帷幕,我们珍惜伟大时代赋予的发展机遇,以首善标准全力提供交通服务保障。智能高效的指挥调度,精准有力的安全预案,暖心贴心的出行服务,我们用实际行动完成冬奥会、冬残奥会交通服务保障任务,诠释了北京公交人的责任与担当,为重大活动交通保障提供了新的标杆。

北京公交被中共中央、国务院授予"北京冬奥会、冬残奥会突出贡献集体"称号

强化组织领导,周密部署落实
成立以集团主要领导为总指挥、班子成员为副总指挥的迎保冬奥总指挥部,抽调精干管理人员和优秀调度员、驾驶员、保修工等执行上会任务

运营服务过硬,措施落实到位
坚持调度机制,加强运行监控;优化行车计划,准发准点率均达到99%以上;加强应急准备,完成了39项应急保障任务

科技引领护航,多措并举发力
以数字科技引领,赋能冬奥保障,实现上会车辆位置、速度、图像等实时动态数据采集的秒级上传,打造冬奥巴士调度系统

牢固底线意识,压实工作责任
全面评估赛事交通保障风险,制定安全应急保障预案;分批组织人员,开展培训演练,提升保障能力;加强过程管控,确保万无一失

参与冬奥会、冬残奥会延庆赛区交通服务保障的驾驶员庄严宣誓

冬奥会、冬残奥会交通服务保障

特殊天气应急演练车辆

冬奥救援保障车辆

案例 非凡行动誓保安全

作为首都国企,北京公交扎实担当起冬奥会、冬残奥会赛事交通服务保障的责任,前后12次组织人员前往小海陀山踏勘线路,绘制小海陀山行车安全示意图,编制《小海陀山山区道路安全通行规定》。积极推进形成特殊天气熔断机制、事故故障闭环处理机制。赛事保障期间,延庆上会团队坚持每天凌晨4点提前上山验路,排查线路安全隐患,制定特殊天气、特殊路段安全行车措施,实现上会保障任务行车安全万无一失和地面常规公交安全大局稳定,圆满完成交通服务保障任务。

延庆赛区上会驾驶员接受山区道路安全行驶培训

听 这雪花说(节选)

——雷超 方元媛

2022年,以立春之日的"一片雪花"
开启了一届简约、安全、精彩的奥运盛会
北京,成为了全球首个双奥之城
每一个精彩瞬间,都让世界为之瞩目
在这场大战大考的保障背后
北京公交这朵"雪花"也是其中一道靓丽的风景

听 这雪花
在冬奥会前夕立下的铮铮誓言
"为出色完成冬奥运输保障任务,作为一名'首都公交驾驶员',我宣誓……"
守最美的风景做最好的保障
"双奥夫妻"王立军、张新静
同在闭环内,却从未见过一次面
在公交人心中,有一种"团聚"叫做同行同往
听 这是如雪花一般的冬奥精神
虽然不是运动员 每个公交人
却也有自己心中的"珠峰"
这"珠峰"是北京2022年冬奥会火炬手
全国劳动模范驾驶员常洪霞
在开幕式上手手相传国旗的那一刻

是服务最高海拔超过一千米
有二十余处"胳膊肘弯"线路的驾驶员张得辉
希望能把这座城市最好的一面展现给世界的那份初衷
万人运输,千车组织,秒级调度,零次失误
冬奥精神锤炼了"世界一流"客运出行服务
也是我们交出的亮眼答卷

听 这雪花
难说再见,已化为一簇炬火
在未来还有更多故事继续诉说

新时代交通人宣讲比赛现场

扫一扫,观看《听 这雪花说》宣讲现场

护航每一次重大活动

我们永葆高度政治责任感和使命感,在党的二十大、全国"两会"、服贸会等重要时期和关键节点,全面宣传动员部署,以最高标准、最强组织、最实举措、最佳状态落实各项保障工作,强化应急值守和突发事件处置,高水平、高质量、高标准完成各项交通服务保障任务。在春节、国庆节、开学季等特殊节点,我们同样提前规划、调度部署,最大程度满足乘客的出行需求。

党的二十大召开期间
日均出动检查人员
261名

检查运营车
2380辆次

案例 精精益求精,万万无一失保障全国"两会"

2022年3月3日上午9:50,随着河北省代表团乘坐的G6732次列车缓缓驶入北京西站,2022年全国人民代表大会接机接站工作全面开启。北汽出租集团从国家大局出发,坚持首善标准,精心准备、精心服务、周密安排,扎实细致地做好各项工作,从会务安排、任务分工、人员选派、车辆保障、会风会纪、优质服务、责任落实等进行了详细规划和部署。整个会议期间,北汽出租集团独家承担了全国人大全部34个代表团、20个驻地和军乐团交通服务保障任务。共计出车6103次,运送乘客58500人次,行李12000多件次,安全行驶里程达207498公里,确保了交通安全万无一失、车辆调派万无一失、优质服务万无一失、治安防范万无一失、疫情防控万无一失,第45次圆满完成了全国人代会交通服务保障任务,向各级领导和全国人民交上了一份满意的答卷。

服务全国"两会"

同心协力抗击疫情

上下同欲者胜,同舟共济者赢。抗疫之战,最稳固的"后盾"是每位乘客的理解支持,最强大的"冲锋"是每位员工的积极配合。北京公交相信只有与广大乘客同心,与员工齐力,才能让从快、从严、从紧的防控力度与更细、更实、更多的人文关怀相辅相成,筑牢疫情防控的坚固屏障。

在阻隔疫情防控风险工作中,累计对

1151条次

线路采取临时调度措施

群防群控,聚合力

疫情防控为了每一个人,也依靠每一个人。在抗击疫情的关键时期,北京公交积极履行公交行业的疫情防控责任,让防疫工作落实到公交运营的每一班次、每一环节,因时因势优化防疫措施,努力为乘客提供放心、安全的乘车环境。

精准迅速
响应调度

全力做好
运输保障

灵活调整
应急预案

2022年5月到6月,为落实市委市政府"让社会面静下来、果断采取措施迅速阻隔疫情防控风险"的要求,快速响应,精准调度,陆续对朝阳区南部、房山区全域、顺义区全域、丰台区全域及其他各区封(管)控周边采取临时调度措施

为了万无一失完成市政府疫情应急运输保障任务,北京公交制定了《应对疫情应急运输保障工作预案》,成立了公交集团应急运输保障总指挥部和前线指挥部,筹集2000辆车、3000名驾驶员、400余名管理及调度人员组建了18个应急车队,其中9个应急运输车队、9个应急备用车队

2022年11月到12月,为落实公交线路"不停运、不断线、不甩站"要求,克服各类管控措施对公交运营的影响,北京公交制定《疫情快速发展情况下地面公交运输保障工作预案》,紧急处置场站、线路的应急情况,科学合理安排运力,助力首都度过第一波感染高峰,全力保障市民出行

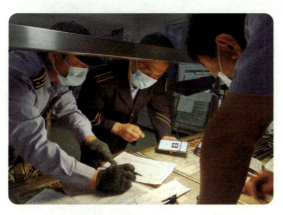

公交驾驶员核验健康码

公交场站开展疫情防控工作

慎终如始，细落实

为筑牢疫情防控坚固防线，北京公交坚持从严从细从实落实疫情防控各项工作，不断完善疫情防控制度体系，有序开展涉疫风险排查、防疫工作检查、疫情防控应急演练，慎终如始做好疫情常态化防控。

健全疫情防控体系

及时制定、更新各项疫情防控文件，制定下发《公交集团疫情防控（简易）操作指南》等疫情防控文件，完善集团公司防疫制度体系；建立完善防疫信息基础台账，及时动态更新，实时跟踪疫情防控信息。

组织开展检查演练

采取定期检查、专项检查的方式，组织开展疫情防控检查工作，全面系统排查各单位疫情防控措施落实情况；策划开展"运营车辆搭载涉疫人员情况下的防控工作推演视频脚本"主题视频演练活动，强化疫情防控各项措施，有力提升疫情防控突发事件应急处置能力。

制定下发疫情防控文件及通知

400余份

撰写疫情防控每日动态信息简报

240期

心系员工，暖人心

我们在疫情防控的过程中持续加强组织关怀，不折不扣地将保障机制、关怀措施一一落实到位，让公交员工在疫情寒冬中不惧风雨，暖心前行。

落实疫情防控保障

- 全面掌握乘务管理员疫苗接种、核酸检测等情况，加强对乘务管理员疫情防控知识和出乘履职培训教育
- 及时、科学调整疫情期间的到岗率和班型，做好后勤保障

开展慰问关怀活动

- 持续关注受疫情影响的困难员工，为员工送去消毒喷雾、免洗凝胶等慰问品
- 关爱下沉干部，工会按照每人300元标准购买防护、生活用品送到他们手中

科学理性认识防疫

- 开展以"科学防疫共克时艰"为主题的防疫知识答题活动，让员工掌握应对疫情的理论知识和防护技能
- 及时了解员工居家工作、生活及心理情况，为员工提供心理疏导、答疑解惑等服务

全系统各级工会设立疫情防控专项资金
1050.26万元

慰问关爱员工
12.28万人次

发放款物
434.22万元

慰问执行小汤山方舱医院运营任务员工

为员工送去防疫物品

共享
携手并进，同创价值

增进民生福祉是发展的根本目的，良好的生态环境与和谐的社会氛围是最普惠的民生福祉。作为首都地面公交的运行主体，北京公交将可持续发展的原则贯穿企业发展始终，坚持以人为本，充分尊重和关怀员工，积极承担国企责任，主动发挥企业自身优势，促进环境、社会的友好和谐发展，携手更多利益相关者参与共享的、持续的价值创造，共同驶向更加美好的未来。

响应联合国可持续发展目标

1 无贫穷

3 良好健康与福祉

5 性别平等

7 经济适用的清洁能源

8 体面工作和经济增长

10 减少不平等

11 可持续城市和社区

13 气候行动

成就每个人的价值

夫济大事必以人为本。北京公交前行的百年征途上,镌刻着拼搏奉献者的足迹,记录着奋进笃行者的步伐。我们与员工共同成长,致力于打造平等、包容、健康的职业平台,让企业的发展成果在得益于广大员工团结奉献的同时,又惠及每一名员工,努力提升员工职业认同感、获得感和幸福感,让每个人的才华充分展现、个人价值得到充分释放,在奋斗中成就精彩人生。

让劳动更加体面

员工是企业实现可持续发展的主体力量。我们严格遵守《中华人民共和国劳动法》等法律法规,坚持平等雇佣,为员工提供有竞争力的薪酬和福利,保障员工的各项基本权益,努力畅通与员工之间的沟通渠道,让员工畅所欲言,让每个人的声音都能被听见。

多元、平等与包容

坚持公开公平的招聘制度,以健全的用工管理体系保障员工的基本权益,推动落实《北京公交集团工作场所反暴力、歧视、性骚扰管理办法》,确保员工拥有平等、安全、健康的工作环境。

完善薪酬激励

坚持足额、按时为员工缴纳五险一金,健全薪酬福利体系,强化奖励机制,加强企业年金管理,让员工的付出与努力得到充分的认可。

重视民主沟通

完善厂务公开民主管理工作机制,召开三届四次、五次职工代表大会,进一步健全职工董事监事工作机制;在"网上职工之家"设立公开专栏,畅通员工诉求表达渠道。

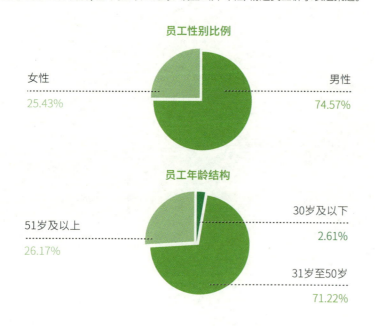

员工性别比例

女性 25.43%　　男性 74.57%

员工年龄结构

51岁及以上 26.17%

30岁及以下 2.61%

31岁至50岁 71.22%

吸纳就业人数
1928人

劳动合同签订率
100%

社会保险覆盖率
100%

人均带薪休假天数
11天

女性管理者比例
40.5%

招聘硕士及以上学历同比增幅
73.7%

引进世界知名院校、国内"双一流"高校毕业生同比增幅
62.5%

相伴而行 迸发活力

我们将员工视为让企业生生不息的种子，以"成人达己"的理念推动员工与企业的共同发展。大力推进交通强国与产教融合试点任务，续航终身职业教育工程，培养高技能人才，充分激发员工潜能和活力，为员工提供施展才华的舞台。

关注人才培养

我们重视人才培养与干部队伍建设，积极挖掘就业岗位，促进高校毕业生就业，引进高素质高质量人才，持续推进人才"启航计划"和管理培训生项目，构建以源头培养为基石，以跟踪培养为手段，以岗位培养为关键的人才培养体系，全面提升人才综合素质能力。

此外，我们整体谋划干部队伍建设，建立起上下贯通、前后接续、良性循环的培养使用体系；实施"基石培养任务""骨干培养任务""拔尖培养任务""头雁培养任务"，努力建设高素质专业化管理人员队伍，大力培养优秀年轻干部，为人才成长成才搭建平台。

强化员工培训

我们深入健全职业教育体制，围绕员工成长各阶段提供全方位的赋能培训，大力推行终身技能训练制度，拓展学习培训渠道、丰富技能培训内容，全面支持员工个人成长与职业发展。

案例 搭建成长平台，培养高技能人才 ——————

为强化技能领军人才队伍建设，北京公交于2022年4月发布《关于开展2022年享受北京市政府技师特殊津贴人员推荐工作的通知》，面向生产、服务一线岗位上业绩突出的技师、高级技师以及集团级及以上技能大师工作室领办人遴选参评人员。经北京市技师特殊津贴评审委员会评审，北京公交客五分公司崔嫚等3人脱颖而出，与本市其他61名技师共同获得"2022年享受北京市政府技师特殊津贴人员"殊荣。

同时，北京公交持续加大对技能人才工作的重视程度和支持力度，通过修订高技能人才管理规定，实行技能大师工作室评审机制，动态管理技能大师工作室梯队，形成工作室"能上能下"的动态管理模式，激发技能人才积极性、主动性、创造性，让各类人才在技能提升和职业发展过程中，奋斗有舞台、发展有空间、事业能出彩。

第四期"常青藤"优秀青年人才训练营

45名青年骨干参训

组织开展各类党员干部培训班

105期

各类党员干部培训班培训人员

2.9万余人次

培训员工

14万人次

培训时数超

4806505小时

"公交云课堂"APP累计激活用户

81551人次

完成

1934名

驾驶员高级企业新型学徒培养工作

成功建立集团级及以上技能大师工作室

17个

其中国家级

1个

北京市级

5个

集团公司级

11个

培养工匠人才

我们倡导尊崇工匠精神的企业风尚,通过创新开展技能认定工作、举办内部兼职讲师培训认证、完善高技能人才培养机制,努力为技能人才搭建宽广舞台,让工匠人才充分展现匠心光彩。

案例

人才"强引擎"谱写公交发展新篇章

2022年7月,北京公交组织开展"十四五"时期内部兼职讲师培训认证暨第四届微课大赛。经过为期四天的课程培训和三天的课题开发,101名学员结合自身岗位实践经验,准确把握课程定位和学习目标,获得微课设计开发能力,自主开发了101门课程,并通过微课大赛展示培训成果。大赛评选出30名优秀学员,颁发优秀讲师证书。育才造士,立企之本。本次培训认证对建设关键岗位胜任模型、畅通员工学习发展路径、萃取组织优秀经验具有重要意义,有助于北京公交建设"师资雄厚、设施先进、管理精益、特色鲜明"的行业一流培训基地。

2022年北京市职工职业技能大赛——道路客运汽车驾驶员(大客车)技能竞赛决赛

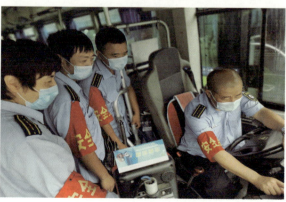

全国五一劳动奖章获得者——客六分公司粘志宽

劳动竞赛实操培训

择一业 终一生

> '择一业，终一生'一直以来都是我信奉的职业理念，在与北京公交同行的二十多年时间里，我不仅见证了集团公司的变迁发展，历经了自己的成长蜕变，更从中真切体会到了企业发展与个人奋斗的同频共振。
>
> ——北京公交客四分公司第一车队1路驾驶员
> 常洪霞

1995年，我正式加入北京公交，从乘客到乘务员，再到驾驶员，日子一天天过去，一路走来，一路成长，一路收获。在磨练驾驶技术的日子里，我感受到公司对员工无处不在的支持和帮助，也总能从同事身上看到一种敬业奉献的执着追求。更重要的是，我切身体会到北京公交在员工的辛勤耕耘下慢慢稳定、发展、壮大，让我对公交文化、公交氛围都产生了深刻的认同感和融入感。

多年来，北京公交坚持稳步推进"人才强企"战略，整合企业优质资源和产业优势资源，为员工成长成才搭建更为广阔的平台。令我印象最深的是2010年，我报名参加了由北京市总工会主办的第一届职工职业技能（大客车）专业比赛，最终取得第九名的成绩。技能大赛帮助我跨越了工作年限要求，实现了自身专业能力的迅速提升，为我个人的职业生涯提供了一个宝贵机会，让我提前6年从中级驾驶员直接晋升为了高级驾驶员，也从中切实体会到了北京公交政策所带来的红利。

北京公交给予我的不仅是技能上的成长，更多的是帮助我确立了人生定位和自我价值的实现路径。2019年，我接过车队创新工作室的大旗，成为了"洪霞创新工作室"的领头人，带领创新工作室的成员，围绕生产经营中的热点、难点创新攻关。我们通过创新工作室把员工内部分散、微小的智慧力量凝聚起来，让集体的创新力量在这一平台上发光发热，努力为乘客带去更智慧、人性化的服务。我希望能继续通过这样的方式，带动更多青年员工走技能之路、创新之路，让员工的才华得到充分施展，让更多创意在车厢"落地生花"。

与公交同行的这一路虽然洒满了汗水，但也充满了最美好、最独特的风景。如今的我，依旧像刚进入公交时那样，用心打磨自己的技艺，一心想把服务做到极致，努力让所学技能都发挥应有的价值。未来，我也希望用自己的人生历程和北京公交一起见证更多城市风景变迁与美好出行的延续。

赤忱关怀暖人心

我们始终将员工视作企业最重要的财富，持续关注、保障员工身心健康，积极帮助员工解决工作生活中遇到的困难，组织开展丰富多彩的业余活动，营造舒适愉悦的工作氛围，让员工深切感受到企业的关爱之情和融融暖意，提升员工幸福感和归属感。

关注员工身心健康

我们有序推进员工健康体检，组织健康讲座与义诊活动，围绕员工心脑血管疾病多发的情况，设计推出"心血管专项健康保障"服务方案，协助员工对重大疾病早检查、早预防。同时关注员工心理健康，针对性开展员工心理疏导，心理适宜性普测，全方位守护员工的身心健康。

冬奥驾驶员心理健康辅导

传递关怀温暖

我们坚持"两确保一降低"困难员工帮扶机制，开展有针对性的慰问活动，为在岗员工夏送凉爽、冬送温暖，将各项实实在在的暖心举措落到实处，将爱与关怀传递给每位员工。

员工体检覆盖率

100%

开展

100名EAP专员培训

组织现场健康讲座与义诊活动

6次

困难员工帮扶资金投入

303.15万元

困难员工帮扶人数

860人

累计成立职工之家

189个

搭建心灵驿站

101个

建成职工书屋

130个

夏送凉爽活动

冬送温暖活动

多彩文体活动

我们广泛组织开展职工文化节、职工嘉年华、公交大集等系列活动，以丰富多彩的文体活动支持员工培养广泛的兴趣爱好，激发员工活力，让员工以轻松、愉悦的心态享受工作与生活。

第四届职工嘉年华　　　　　　丰富多彩的员工活动　　　　　公交大集活动

好书悦享会　　　　　　　　　　"送你一朵小红花"活动

企业文化凝心聚力

积淀百年情怀的北京公交，承载着"一路同行　一心为您"的最美初心。我们高度重视企业文化建设、新闻宣传与品牌建设，开展线上线下宣讲，展示丰富文创产品，组织特色互动活动，传递公交故事，唱响文化品牌，为集团公司"十四五"发展规划实施和企业高质量发展提供强大的文化动力。

同行文化兰州演出活动

同行文化品牌展台

北京公交企业文化手册

公交系列盲盒

扫一扫，观看"北京公交
同行文化兰州展演"

藏在镜头背后的人

> 镜头呈现出来的，是一幕幕精彩动人的定格时刻；背后付出的，却是从不轻松的辛劳。
>
> ——北京公交宣传部业务主管
> 王超

影像是凝固的时间印记，是化瞬间为永恒的使者。作为一名从基层乘务员成长起来的宣传工作者，王超深知"镜头如同桥梁，不只是与乘客之间，也是与员工之间的桥梁，用镜头更好地展现员工的风采，让更多的人了解不一样的北京公交"。他是这么说，也是这么做的。在北京公交，王超是抗击疫情、新中国成立70周年庆祝活动、北京2022年冬奥会和冬残奥会等重大活动交通服务保障背后的记录者，是公交车载视频、员工休息室、调度室电视节目的制作者。在公交之外，王超也是北京市广播电视局指导的纪录片《一路百年》、中央新影集团承制的电影《一路幸福》等作品的视频素材贡献者。"冬奥期间我有幸来到延庆赛区的小海陀山，看见远处盘山路上，一辆辆公交车缓缓行驶，背景是高山雪道，激动之下迅速爬上身边高台，一脚踩空险些摔伤，但顾不了太多了。回到家时，脸上又痒又疼，后来才知道，还有冻脱皮这一说。"王超感慨道。扛起相机、选择位置、架好机位、找好角度、变换光线、切换构图……每一幕、每一帧背后，都是漫长的等待守候和适时地按下快门。

2023年2月，王超荣获第九届"国企好新闻"新闻创客提名奖，这是对他个人价值和千万作品的充分肯定。为重大活动记录，为公交人发声，为企业传播，这也是在新媒体时代，无数像王超一样的公交人在摸爬滚打中逐步变得游刃有余的技能，从未改变的公交情怀指引着他们为企业文化宣传尽心尽力，传递出更加负责任有担当的企业品牌形象。

环境友好绿色出行

在"双碳"目标背景下，绿色出行成为行业共识。碧水蓝天，洁净空气，鸟语花香，是人们对生活环境的希冀，也是北京公交对绿色交通、绿色出行的深刻实践。北京公交调整车辆结构，推进节能减排，吸引更多市民乘坐公交，提高公共交通出行分担率，带来更加洁净清新的出行环境，提供全新的绿色出行体验，以绿色驱动可持续未来。

公交为城市"添绿"

我们逐步调整优化车辆能源结构，大力推广使用纯电动车、增程式混合动力电动车等，努力提升车辆利用效率，减少低效、无效公里投放，降低资源消耗。同时加强充电桩、加氢站等配套设施建设，让每一辆公交车乘着清洁之风在街巷穿行、在城市中流动。

氢能源公交车

清洁能源和新能源公交车占比

94.27%

氢能源公交车

217辆

更新购置新能源公交车

2220辆

建成加氢站

2座

在225处公交场站内建设完成充电桩

1524台

案例 投入运营新能源公交车，助力城市绿色发展

为加快改善环境空气质量，进一步增强人民群众蓝天幸福感，持续打赢蓝天保卫战，北京公交将车辆能源结构持续向新能源倾斜，投入运营氢能源公交车。与传统能源公交车相比，新能源公交车在车辆外观、结构设计等方面都有突出特色，具有启动平稳、噪音小、排放少、节能环保等优点，既为广大乘客提供了安全、绿色、便捷的出行服务，也让城市变得更宜居。

能源消耗总量

418298 吨标准煤

能耗强度

4.36 吨标准煤/万公里

碳排放交易

11.41 万吨

净收益

1165.02 万元

让清新蔚蓝常驻

我们积极助力首都空气质量持续向好,建立健全各项节能降耗管理制度、车辆能耗指标体系,严格控制运营车辆尾气排放,加大对漆雾、废水、酸雾、粉尘等污染的治理和监管力度,开展固体废弃物环保回收,逐步淘汰改造高耗能设备,助力车辆向零排放迈进,为首都"载来"更加蔚蓝无暇的天空、更加清新舒适的城市面貌。

2020—2022年污染物排放统计表

指标	2020年	2021年	2022年
碳排放量（吨）	275587	288376	246261
二氧化碳排放量（吨）	1010484	1057378	902957
氮氧化物减排量（吨）	186.25	123.41	57.05
颗粒物减排量（吨）	0.41	0.17	0.13
碳氢化合物减排量（吨）	40.93	80.78	30.72

做低碳出行的风向标

绿色行动在细枝末节，在每个点滴。我们拓宽环保行动的履责范围，通过垃圾分类、绿色场站、绿色出行等，积极做绿色发展的宣传者、倡导者、践行者，让低碳成为习惯，努力营造简约适度、绿色低碳的社会风尚，共同守护绿水蓝天的美丽家园。

完成垃圾分类培训教育
4256次

参与培训人数
221916人次

参与场站"桶前值守"比例
100%

义务植树
27.75万株

开展绿色出行站台宣传活动

加强绿色出行宣传

积极开展绿色出行宣传月和公交出行宣传周活动，传递绿色出行新理念，培育绿色出行文化，引导市民选择绿色、文明、低碳出行的方式

场站建设绿色环保

建筑设计执行北京市绿色建筑二星标准，使用绿色环保材料，提高建筑节能效果，公交场站建设采取双喷淋+作业面湿法作业等环保降尘措施以及地下降水二次利用的节水措施

推进垃圾分类

积极推进落实各场站垃圾分类工作，建立管理台账，开展生活垃圾分类示范创建工作，引导广大员工争做垃圾分类的宣传者、引导者、践行者和推动者

积极倡导绿色办公

节约每一张纸、每一度电、每一滴水、每一粒粮；爱惜保管办公用品，减少更换频率；充分利用可循环使用的资源；保持办公卫生，适当绿化

为社区留下长久感动

上善若水,润泽民生。北京公交秉持"一心为乘客、服务最光荣、真情献社会、责任勇担当"的公交精神,把履行社会责任扛在肩上、放在心上、落实在行动上,让文明风尚成为奋勇前行的丰厚滋养,努力打造可持续的供应链管理,常态化开展各项志愿活动,汇聚慈善力量,传递社会温暖,让社区的幸福更可感知、更可触及,创造可持续的社会价值。

崇文门公交便民驿栈

文明同行 美好出行

每一个人既是文明交通的参与者,也是践行者,为营造更加文明有序的出行环境,我们深入开展"文明驾车 礼让行人"专项行动,组织员工积极参与"我承诺我礼让"接力、"文明守法 平安回家"等宣传活动,联合启动"倡导安全骑行 创建文明交通新格局"活动,让文明出行成为一种新风尚。

开展文明出行宣传活动

 案例 倡导安全骑行新风尚 创建文明交通新格局

2022年8月,北京公交驾校联合北京公安局大兴分局交通支队、《摩托车》杂志共同举办"倡导安全骑行新风尚 创建文明交通新格局"系列活动,正式启动2022年摩托车安全骑行季与"2022年摩托车安全骑行季赋能行动",引导驾驶人守好安全行车"生命线",提升广大交通参与者文明交通安全意识。

"倡导安全骑行新风尚 创建文明交通新格局"活动启动仪式

案例 "文明驾车 礼让行人"，助力首都构建文明畅通交通环境

2022年6月10日，由首都精神文明建设委员会办公室联合相关单位开展的"文明驾车 礼让行人——我承诺 我礼让"接力活动举行启动仪式，北汽出租集团作为出租行业代表在分会场参加启动仪式，驾驶员刘韶山、敬清波作为代表向首都同行发出遵守交通法规、礼让斑马线的倡议和承诺，共同为营造文明、安全、有序的首都交通秩序作出贡献。

驾驶员代表发出倡议和承诺

打造可持续供应链

我们与供应商建立紧密、互信、和谐的合作关系，持续推进负责任采购，健全供应商管理制度体系，提高供应商的履责能力，打造诚信、合规、可持续供应链。

 供应商准入与退出

- 以健全的供应商管理制度促进供应商准入与退出机制的科学合理
- 以严谨完善的采购流程与考核制度最大程度降低外部风险的不良影响

 供应商动态管理

- 建立供应商考核评价体系，实现供应商管理的"动态考核"
- 通过公开招标、择优评选等组建供应商企业库

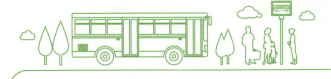

 供应商赋能

- 为企业库内供应商开展业务培训，总结供应商产品质量与服务情况，沟通反馈问题并开展专题培训

供应商管理举措

传递志愿温暖力量

我们始终与公益为伴,主动承担社会责任、积极回馈社会,携手公交青年志愿者开展学雷锋志愿服务等常态化活动,自觉主动进行站杆站牌检查清理等,积极发动志愿者对各项重大活动保障需求做出响应,让点滴力量汇聚温暖光芒,为社会注入更多温情和暖意。

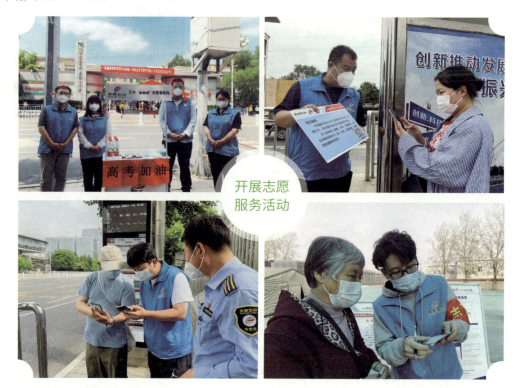

开展志愿服务活动

案例 公交"模范小夫妻",邻里和睦好邻居

陈萌、刘然是一对"80后"公交夫妻,在客三分公司专67路当驾驶员,他们不仅在工作中相互支持、彼此鼓励、敬业爱岗,在生活中更是热心公益、助人为乐,积极参与志愿服务活动,用执着与坚守诠释着"奉献 友爱 互助 进步"的志愿精神。

陈萌、刘然两人孝老爱亲,与邻为善,经常帮助社区老人搬东西,照顾行动不便的邻居。为助力社区做好垃圾分类工作,他们报名成为社区第一批垃圾分类志愿者,并利用手机APP和各种媒体学习垃圾分类知识,耐心为社区居民解答各种疑问。2022年,他们累计参加社区志愿服务活动70余次,自2018年注册成为北京志愿者以来,累计参与志愿服务时长达561小时,他们用自己的真诚和行动,为城市运行和民生保障贡献着自己的力量。

志愿者注册人数
15000余人

志愿服务
20余万人次

志愿服务活动
5.2万次

累计服务时长
73万小时

共托乡村振兴新希望

共护诗画万里路,同筑百年乡村梦。我们加强日常协调统筹,做好巩固拓展脱贫攻坚成果同乡村振兴有效衔接各项工作,以更有力的举措、汇聚更强大的力量,促进农业高质高效、乡村宜居宜业、农民富裕富足,携手多方共同筑梦乡村,接续新程。

支援重点帮扶地区

我们坚持做好东西部协作、对口支援、区域合作等重点任务,结合企业主业工作实际,在产业帮扶、消费帮扶、就业帮扶等方面发力,努力筑牢拓展脱贫攻坚成果,推动受援地区乡村振兴有效衔接。

向内蒙古产业帮扶项目
捐赠资金
100 万元

采购对口帮扶脱贫地区
农副产品
862 万元

向拉萨、乌鲁木齐等地区
捐赠防疫物资
3 万元

帮扶中西部22个省份农
村劳动力稳岗就业
1601 人

向高铺村捐赠防疫物资

客八分公司帮扶黄岭西村购买农产品

产业帮扶

通过捐赠为重点帮扶县内蒙古呼伦贝尔市鄂伦春旗乡村振兴产业帮扶项目菜沫厂购置生产设备,支持完善当地联农带农机制

消费帮扶

引导集团公司各单位采购对口帮扶内蒙古、新疆和田、西藏拉萨等经济不发达地区农副产品

就业帮扶

内蒙古乌鲁布铁镇铁东村产业帮扶项目带动当地50名农民就业增收

帮扶中西部22个省份农村劳动力在公交系统稳岗就业

教育帮扶

公交技校招录西部地区农村人口进行职业学历教育

物资捐赠

向拉萨、乌鲁木齐经济不发达地区捐赠防疫物资,助力当地打赢疫情防控阻击战

新招入
311名
东西部协作省份农村初中毕业生到公交技校进行学历职业教育

招聘退役大学生士兵
20名

新安置北京市农村劳动力就业人数
236人

选派
1名
高级管理人员作为北京市第十批援藏干部,参加为期三年的对口支援西藏工作

帮扶经济薄弱村

我们紧盯定点帮扶北京市门头沟区斋堂镇三个集体经济薄弱村的"消薄"工作,提前完成第一阶段帮扶任务,推动乡村振兴取得新进展、农业农村现代化迈出新步伐。

提前完成"消薄"帮扶任务

- 在黄岭西村聚焦产业帮扶,帮扶建设村史馆,提升旅游发展水平
- 在高铺村开展"学好党史助力乡村振兴"主题党课活动、斋堂文旅进公交车厢宣传活动
- 为法城村村委会添置办公用品,采购法城蜂蜜,帮扶流转闲置农宅

"村村通"公交便利村民出行

- 为定点帮扶的斋堂镇集体经济薄弱村高铺村增设站位,将892路等6条公交线路双向新加"高铺新村"站,方便山区村民出行

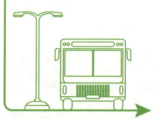

增设"高铺新村"站位

帮扶黄岭西村建设村史馆

衔接乡村幸福路

> 路虽崎岖，道虽遥远，我们始终用爱伴随出行路，满载憧憬与希望，为村民带来更加富裕、幸福的生活。
>
> ——北京公交客八分公司运营管理部副经理
> 殷军辉

北京公交在过去十多年的时间里，不断增加线网、站点的覆盖和服务范围，让山里的村民抬起脚就能走出大山，也将身在都市的人们载向风景如画的山林，一道道车辙加速大山里的农产品运输、助力乡村旅游发展，也在循环往复中拉近了大山与都市间的距离。

我是客八分公司的殷军辉，参与了"村村通"项目从设计规划到线路开通的各个环节。公交人都知道"村村通"公交车实施起来其实是非常具有挑战性的。新通车的村子，绝大多数都是人口较少、山高路远的深山村，一些村子只有十几户人家，路窄崎岖，仅能容一辆小型汽车通行，并不具备大型客车进村的条件。为此，我们积极与各级政府协商，为部分乡村道路加装防护栏杆，协调北京公交内部租赁更多适宜山区出行的车辆，以实现通行条件，力求线路最大程度地覆盖更多村庄。同时，我们还深入各个村落、乡镇，开展村镇级座谈会等调研活动，倾听村民需求，了解村民出行习惯，努力设计出最贴合村民出行需求的站点和线路。

"村村通"公交，满足的不仅仅是山区百姓出行的基本需要，更带动了山区各方面的发展。Y16路公交线路延长至汉家川，让汉家川地区首次通上了公交车，村民可一站直达延庆城区，便利了7个村庄1400多位村民的出行。在村级小型欢迎仪式上，村支部书记赵有刚十分欣喜地说道："我今天非常高兴、非常激动，从今天起，我们去永宁、去延庆城区再也不用挤接驳车了。以后我们村民出行方便了，这儿的核桃、栗子等农产品也可以方便带出去卖了，还能卖上好价钱。"

如今，北京公交依旧用心探索服务山区百姓出行、助力乡村振兴的更多可能。2022年11月，北京公交与中国邮政集团有限公司北京市分公司签署战略合作协议，希望与北京邮政携手，发挥运力、场地等资源优势，增强末端服务能力，畅通工业品下乡和农产品进城双向流通渠道，共同在助力乡村振兴的"国之大者"上贡献更大力量，让爱在大山中继续蔓延。

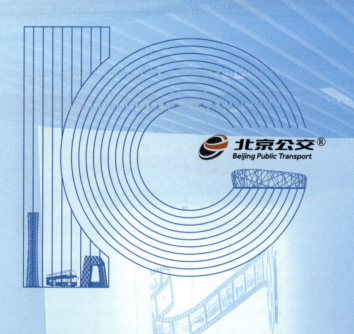

未来
一路同行，向可持续

站在百年新起点，重整行装再出发。新的图景已经绘就，面向第二个百年，北京公交将更加鲜明地展现"以人为本、乘客至上、创新发展、追求卓越"的核心价值观，坚持一心为民谋福祉，勇逐数字化浪潮，推动现代信息技术在公共交通全要素、全领域、全流程的深度融合和广泛应用，乘势新基建，集聚优势产业和各类创新要素，携手各方，步调一致地朝着新的目标奋勇前进，把宏伟蓝图变为美好现实。

响应联合国可持续发展目标

9 产业、创新和基础设施

11 可持续城市和社区

12 负责任消费和生产

怀着初心出发 启航美好出行

——北京市交通委员会地面公交运营管理处原处长 王昊

北京市交通委员会
地面公交运营管理处原处长 王昊

百年光辉的历史征程中，作为与首都百姓生活最贴近的公共出行服务企业，北京公交积极回应时代命题，在智慧调度、安全出行、大型活动保障等方面竭心尽力，为服务首都公共交通建设，带动区域经济社会发展，推动落实交通强国战略作出了卓越贡献。

首都公交是全国公交的榜样和标杆，站在新的十年，更是新的百年的起点上，应当坚守初心不负众望，用更广阔的视野和更有力的举措向现代城市客运出行综合服务商的目标迈进。

2020年，《北京市地面公交线网总体规划》正式发布。三年来，北京公交围绕总体规划要求进行线路优化，"3+1"的线网体系已初步形成，尤其2021年围绕轨道站点接驳等采取了多项行动，成效显著。近几年，受疫情影响，公交客运量有所下降，这需要北京公交认真思考，不断提高运营服务水平和效率，加强宣传，保证乘客乘坐公交车有更好的体验，增强地面公交的吸引力。

随着"双碳"目标的提出，经济与环境的协调发展被提升到了新的高度。特别是对于首都来说，城市绿色底色关乎城市品质，关乎民生福祉，更关乎国家形象。北京公交从2012年开始，就陆续在减少传统燃料公交车的应用，车型历经多次迭代升级，变得更加低碳环保。未来需要进一步降低成本，减少空驶里程，合理布局充电设施，打好提质增效组合拳，真正实现绿色转型。

- -

公共交通领域涉及多主体、多要素，促进交通领域的综合发展至关重要，构建健康可持续的公共交通生态系统势在必行。

近期，市交通委与北京交通广播合作开设的"治堵大家谈"栏目正式更名为"交通大家谈"，这更突出了各种交通出行方式融合发展的必要性。未来，北京公交更需与多方合作，加强沟通，相辅相成，互相支持，让各种交通方式发展并行不悖，促进交通领域综合治理。

今年是北京公交第十年发布社会责任报告，意义非凡，下一个十年，希望北京公交更加积极主动，更加灵活多样，在与各方的洽商合作中，推动公共交通行业驶向更美好的未来。

并肩同行 共赴精彩

——国际公共交通联会(UITP)巴士运输部总监 阿诺·克霍夫

2021年11月12日,由北京公交主办的中国(北京)国际公共交通大会召开,会上,UITP秘书长穆罕默德•梅兹甘尼盛赞"北京公交不仅是亚太地区更是全世界的榜样",对此我也表示无比认可和赞同。

UITP巴士运输部总监 阿诺·克霍夫

在奔赴可持续交通的道路上,北京公交一直是我们亲密的合作伙伴和忠实的支持者。

从2017年开始,我们就组织参观团,考察北京公交的智能调度系统、双源无轨电车、充电桩等设施设备。在世界巴士大会等多次会议和国际学术交流活动中,我们都能看到北京公交的风采。2022年,我们与北京公交签署战略合作框架协议,开始筹建UITP北京代表处。今年,新任的UITP亚太分会总监已经就位,我们非常期待与北京公交一起,加强与中国UITP成员和利益相关方的联系,推动公共交通朝着更加绿色、安全、高效、智慧、可持续的方向发展。值得一提的是,北京公交还参与了UITP巴士委员会关于全球公交线网规划最佳实践的项目,项目成果中展示了北京公交多层次的线网体系,这是非常好的超大城市线网规划的示例。

- -

多年的合作交流中,北京公交一直坚守着作为巴士委员会委员单位的职责,在中国积极发挥引领带动作用,推动公交行业的可持续发展。

如今,公共交通领域的发展重点已经发生了变化,随着气候变化的危机愈演愈烈,所有公交企业都面临着改善城市环境,推动出行向公共交通方式转变的挑战。据我所知,北京公交目前的清洁能源和新能源公交车占比已经达到了90%以上,这对改善空气质量、提升环保效益作出了巨大的贡献,我想这也是所有公交企业需要努力的方向。作为公交行业的一员,我们真切希望城市更清洁、更健康、更宜居。

未来,我们非常期待与北京公交有更多更深入的交流与沟通,促进国际公共交通政策、制度、规则、标准、技术互学互鉴,共同为构建更加现代化、更加节能环保、更加人本友好的可持续公共交通付诸努力。

城市更新，让"老地方"焕发新活力

北京公交积极融入首都发展新格局，在北京大力实施城市更新行动背景下，利用闲置场站空间协站资源，推动"腾笼换鸟"和品质提升，打造"1921城市智享空间"系列园区，实现存量空间资源提质增效，织补多元城市服务功能，为首都城市更新作出贡献。

整合空间资源，抓好顶层设计。

北京公交坚持严控增量和疏解存量相结合，将中心城区大型驻车、维修、保养等功能外移，腾退出一批承载北京公交文化基因和历史职能的场站空间。同时，提出"利用场站空间服务首都功能、提升城市品质"的思路，打造"1921城市智享空间"系列项目规划。

完善推进机制，统筹推动实施。

为加快项目落地建设，北京公交组建成立"1921城市智享空间"重大项目专班，统筹协调难点问题，定期调度项目进度；设立北京公交集团城市更新运营管理有限公司，作为延伸城市公共服务功能、助力产业结构提质升级的专职经营主体；组建北京城市空间投资管理有限公司等，负责试点项目的投资、建设、运营。

加快建设步伐，塑立公交品牌。

北京公交参与改造的东城区花园胡同园区已投入运营，使老旧楼宇院落焕发出现代化智能化园区的新风貌，入驻率超过90%；全面改造南礼士路园区，形成全新学院派建筑外观；新风街3号项目完成设计规划，纳入西城区城市更新重点项目。

花园胡同园区　　　　　　　　　　　　南礼士路园区

未来，"1921"系列园区将按照"两年一周期、整体三步走"的阶段安排，有计划、有步骤地推进更新改造，努力建成一批集公共服务、在地文化、商业场景相融合的多元化公共空间，塑造北京公交城市更新事业的特色品牌。

打造标准化建设新高地

2022年11月，北京公交标准化试点项目——"北京地面公共交通运营服务标准化试点"以97.5的高分成功通过终期评估验收，这是北京市公共交通标准化发展迈出的重要一步，具有里程碑意义。北京市交通委、北京市市场监管局联合发布政务信息，充分肯定了集团公司标准化建设工作。标准化工作是建设现代公交企业的重要内容，是全面提升企业经营管理、服务质量和服务水平的重要方式，在推进企业治理体系和治理能力现代化中发挥着基础性、引领性作用。

早在"十二五"时期，集团公司明确提出，要向着标准化、精细化、信息化、现代化方向大步迈进。2020年3月至2022年3月，我们作为国家级第六批社会管理和公共服务综合标准化试点建设单位，承担起北京地面公共交通运营服务标准化试点项目建设工作。

重任在前，我们无所畏惧；责任在肩，我们细致落实。

我们围绕标准化试点建设的各项目标任务，坚持"标准化、数字化、精细化"发展思路，高点定位、高标推进、高效落实。我们加强标准化顶层设计，成立试点工作领导小组，统筹谋划标准化发展重大事项。印发《标准化试点项目建设实施方案》，搭建集团公司标准体系。逐步优化标准化工作流程，推动标准机制、标准能力和标准文化协调发展，深入标准宣贯与实施评估，改变了过去制度代替标准的"准标准化"管理模式，达到了"形与实"的双重标准化管理，标准化工作从经验型向专业型转变、从部分标准化向整体标准化转变。过去三年，我们累计发布41项企业标准、2项团体标准，修订1项北京市地方标准。2022年，集团公司公益性单位节约资金5.45亿元，超额完成既定任务目标，运营调度、服务保障、安全稳定、改革创新等质量得到新的提升。

标准化建设工作只有进行时，没有完成时。

未来三年，我们将以打造"1+4+N"的北京公交标准化发展新格局为总体工作目标，聚焦生产经营和基础管理两大重点领域，提高企业标准创制水平，同时坚持闭环管理，形成"整改—落实—提升"的良好局面，加强协同联动、交流互鉴，努力打造北京公交标准品牌，推动标准化工作向更广领域、更深层次和更高水平迈进，为集团公司改革发展再立新功、再创佳绩。

北京地面公共交通运营服务标准化试点终期考核评估会

评估组专家现场观看智能调度系统操作演示

领跑自动驾驶新赛道

随着汽车产业与人工智能、物联网、高性能计算等新一代信息技术深度融合，自动驾驶逐渐成为全球汽车与交通出行领域智能化和网联化发展的方向。

在这场科技浪潮中，北京公交积极着眼自动驾驶前沿科技和未来智能交通发展战略布局，形成自动驾驶解决方案，为企业改革发展打造新的动能引擎。

2017年8月，我们与Mobileye视觉科技有限公司合作，在4条公交线路试点安装主动安全预警系统，推动公交从传统被动安全技术向智能主动安全技术蜕变。我们抓住北京冬奥会的契机，与丰田公司展开合作，于2022年1月至3月在冬奥赛区首钢园区进行自动驾驶载客试运营，累计发班293车次、运营2057公里，载客13451人次，积累了自动驾驶公交运营服务经验。2022年11月，我们与北汽福田、轻舟智航、公交准点研究院等产学研用单位对接，签订五方合作协议，集车路协同和单车智能技术路线于一身、长8.5米的首车已完成生产。车身长度、车辆自重和总重的增加，要求技术控制更加精准，我们在自动驾驶公交测试领域实现了一次大跨越、大提升。

"自动驾驶是为未来布局的产业，是科技赋能公交的体现，更是建设现代化公交企业、实现组织创新的必由之路。"

正如战略和改革发展部经理、北京公交高级别自动驾驶示范区建设专项工作组秘书长徐正祥所说，全球科技已经发展到以数字化技术为代表的第四次科技革命，发展自动驾驶不仅有利于降低驾驶员的劳动强度，提高行车安全水平，同时通过对人、车、线、站要素的高度匹配，为乘客打造沉浸式的体验场景，提升公交车的通行效率，缓解交通拥堵，进一步助力交通强国建设。

面向未来，我们将把握北京市高级别自动驾驶示范区和智能网联化城市道路建设的重大机遇，建立健全自动驾驶运营服务机制、流程、标准，持续研究完善公交智能网联、自动驾驶解决方案，积淀自动驾驶领域资源，扩大行业影响，为打造国内领先、世界一流的现代城市客运出行综合服务商的目标添薪蓄力。

与丰田公司合作自动驾驶载客试运营

自动驾驶安全员培训

自动驾驶车辆乘务安全员培训

自动驾驶车辆点检员培训

建设新型公交智库

博士后是具有深厚知识基础和探索创新能力的高层次人才群体,是创新驱动发展战略的重要人才支撑。面对当前地面公共交通在数字化转型、智能调度应用等方面存在的现实问题,我们以"人才强企"发展战略为引领,于2020年成功设立全国首个公交行业博士后科研工作站,开启公交行业建设博士后科研工作站先河。建设博士后科研工作站对集团公司具有重大的战略意义,集团公司要求上下增强建设好博士后科研工作站的责任感、使命感,共同把博士后科研工作站建设成为具有全球视野走在世界前列的新型公交智库和高端智库。

体制新,人才聚;机制顺,活力增。

两年来,我们逐步建立健全博士后科研工作站各项制度机制,面向多专业多领域招聘选拔人才,针对企业发展中的痛点难点问题开展博士后研究课题管理,初步建立计划研究项目库。同时积极与北京航空航天大学、北京理工大学、同济大学、西安交通大学等拥有交通运输、企业管理、法学等相关一级学科博士授予权的高等院校博士后流动站进行沟通,广泛开展联合培养高校库建设,筑起丰富的运营场景和良好的研究平台之巢,吸引众多优秀人才来此落地生根。2022年,博士后科研工作站累计接收简历70份,面试30场(次)、41人次。2022年新入站博士后郑营表示:"北京公交具有丰富的应用场景,累积了海量数据资源,作为博士后工作站科研人员,我希望充分利用平台优势,把理论基础和公交运营实际有机结合,深入学习调研,强化务实创新,推动成果转化,为北京公交高质量发展贡献力量。""北京公交在数字化信息化、自动驾驶方面有非常前沿的尝试,这驱使着我从人工智能、从自动驾驶入手,去研究对公共交通政策法规的影响。未来希望进一步深入研究,促进公共交通的智能化、规范化发展。"2022年新入站博士后李贝妮说道。

功以才成,业由才广。

正如集团战略和改革发展部经理、博士后科研工作站秘书长徐正祥所言:"建立博士后科研工作站,就是通过扩大生态圈,生动深刻地剖析公交的痛点难点问题以及前沿发展方向,把过去碎片化的经验上升到系统化理论化的高度,使公交从传统企业变成创新型企业。"站在新的百年起点上,我们也将充分发挥博士后制度优势,补齐差距,把握机遇,使博士后人才在赋能传统公交转型升级和高质量发展中发挥更大的实质性的支持作用。同时与各方携手,全力打造全国示范性公交行业产、学、研、用协同创新基地,扩大公交生态圈,开创人才发展新局面。

北京公交集团博士后科研工作站管理委员会第一次（扩大）会议召开

北京公交集团领导接见首批进站博士后研究人员

可持续的公交 可持续的未来

百年来，老一辈北京公交人树起的华灯照亮了砥砺前行的来时路，而被华灯点亮的新时代北京公交人，将继续以诚挚的心不断创造可持续的价值，擘画未来公交的可持续发展图景。

交通是影响全球可持续发展的重要领域，可持续的交通对贡献联合国可持续发展目标至关重要。联合国可持续发展目标11提出，到2030年，向所有人提供安全、负担得起、无障碍和可持续的运输系统，改进道路安全，扩大公共交通。然而根据联合国的发布《2022年可持续发展目标报告》，目标11中指出"世界上只有大约一半的城市居民享有便捷的公共交通，在寻求提高无障碍、包容、安全、可靠和高效的公共交通系统的供应和使用方面，仍面临着大量的工作"。未来，公共交通领域的发展仍将面临压力与动力共生、机遇与挑战并存的局面。

我们一直置身于可持续发展的大背景中，深刻对标联合国可持续发展目标，不断丰富城市客运出行服务内涵，拓展服务空间，提高服务能力，不断审视思考如何在时代发展的潮流中既靠得住，又有所为，携带"为民"的社会责任基因，基于自身专业发展优势，以可持续公交助力可持续发展。

北京公交责任理念与贡献的 SDGs 目标

公交是城市的公交，是人民的公交。随着北京城市空间结构及人口结构的变化，打造开放、包容的未来公交系统将是我们不断追求的目标。我们将正确把握"首都""城市"和"交通"的关系、"疏解""联动"和"突破"的关系，主动融入首都城市新发展，为融入京津冀城市群建设、推进公共交通导向的城市发展(TOD)模式贡献北京公交方案。同时，我们将持续升级自身服务，并与其他出行服务高效衔接、有机融合。在充分准确把握民众对出行的便捷性、多样性、无碍性、包容性、舒适性、安全性等新趋势和新要求的基础上，持续深化地面公交供给侧结构性改革，形成需求牵引供给、供给创造需求的城市客运出行综合服务新模式。

数字经济正驱动着百行百业的变革新生，数字化、智能化将成为未来公交系统高效、可持续发展的关键。未来，我们将同步推进智能车辆、智慧管理、智慧调度等，释放数字化转型在生产、运营、管理、服务等各领域各环节的放大、叠加、倍增效应，依托海量数据，实时精准穿透生产经营状况和乘客出行需求，推动公交运营产品与服务不断迭代更新，实现科技赋能、智慧决策、精准施策，不断提高公交运行效率和服务水平，引领公交行业创新发展和可持续发展。

在能源、气候的双重约束下，绿色出行、低碳交通将是实现"双碳"目标的关键，这也将是未来交通发展的主要方向，在这一趋势下，公共交通在城市交通系统中的主导地位将进一步被强化。作为首都地面公交的服务主体，在大力发展绿色低碳装备、调整车辆结构、促进车辆更新的同时，我们将加快配套设施建设，减少汽油、柴油等化石能源消耗，全面推行清洁生产，积极开展节能减排核算和碳排放交易，以更清晰的量化指标展现对低碳目标的支持。同时，提高公交吸引力和竞争力，让公交的便捷符合人们的期望和预期，切实推动人们出行结构的调整，让公交成为人们出行的首选，这也将是我们未来构建绿色公交、贡献绿色交通的主要着力点。

我们亦深知未来需要各方共同着墨，期待与多方联动、合力推进，携手共同推进中国交通事业向纵深发展。

正如道路一直向前，我们将一直向未来，可持续。

展望

百年前，一声"铛铛车"的清脆铃声，唤醒了北京公交的世纪之音。百年后，初声依旧，北京公交以越己者恒越的坚实步伐，在时代的坐标里锚定未来。从第十载履责报告再出发，心怀初心使命与各方继续一路同行，于全面贯彻落实党的二十大精神开局之年，科学把握战略机遇和风险挑战，以首善标准开创首都公交事业发展新局面。

与乘客对话，提升出行服务品质

践行"出行即生活"，深化地面公交供给侧结构性改革，构建首都高质量公交线网体系。以出行全过程体验为本，实施灵活高效的调度指挥，提供实时信息服务，持续优化公交供给。创新服务模式，兼顾不同群体的出行需求，发展多样化响应式公交。提升白洋淀水上交通出行服务水平，改善水上交通环境，推动白洋淀"水上巴士"运营。全力推动品牌线路培育建设，以文化滋养提升品牌价值。打造全龄友好的出行环境，让公交出行更具包容性。坚持开放协调共享的发展理念，利用场站资源，帮助解决停车、充电等民生问题，将便民惠民落到实处。

与科技对话，驱动长效创新发展

系统谋划公交自动驾驶发展路径，主动参与北京市高级别自动驾驶示范区建设。开发布局新业态，对接新技术，创新推动破圈发展。以数字化转型释放强大势能，推动公交基础设施数字化、车辆装备智能化、管理服务信息化，集成"人、车、路、网、云、数"转化为企业改革创新发展的新动能和新实力，打造公共交通行业数字化转型的"北京样板"。

与人才对话,增强核心竞争能力

纵深推进人才强企战略,涵养人才蓄水池,打造专业合理的人才梯队,培育高质量发展新优势。以博士后科研工作站为创新平台,精准培育具有现代城市公共交通理念、专业实践能力的跨学科、复合型、战略型、高层次创新型人才。以建设技师学院为抓手,培养选拔公交主体岗位技能劳动者,着力培育更多公交工匠。

与行业对话,引领构建产业生态

发挥行业表率作用,坚守行业科研责任,研判行业重点难点问题,破解行业发展现实困境,引领行业前沿发展方向。以共商共建共享原则,着力发展国内国际产业生态圈,撬动全产业链发展活力,构建互融互通、共创共享的公交新生态系统。

与时代对话,彰显公共交通价值

坚持以首都发展为统领,串联京津冀城市群交通,形成与首都战略定位和京津冀协同发展相匹配的地面公交发展新格局。探索交邮运输合作,共同保障"人享其行、物畅其流",助力乡村振兴。在"双碳"目标下,以公交优先、低碳出行为牵引,增强公共交通吸引力,让更多的人选择公交绿色出行,提高公共交通出行分担率。打造公交行业国际交往中心,以"交通天下"的姿态向世界递出北京公交名片。

新征程是充满光荣和梦想的远征,我们将步履坚定,始终保持与乘客同频,与时代同行,向打造国内领先、世界一流的现代城市客运出行综合服务商的目标踔厉奋发、笃行不怠,开创北京公交更加美好的明天!

关键绩效

	指标	2020年	2021年	2022年
经济绩效	仟营业收入（亿元）	74.58	81.91	68.61
	企业总资产（亿元）	651.79	645.21	643.27
	企业净资产（亿元）	410.72	423.55	444.10
	资产负债率（%）	36.99	32.08	30.92
	纳税总额（亿元）	3.40	4.15	2.89
	运营车辆（辆）	34025	32896	32783
	运营线路条数（条）	1214	1225	1299
	公共电汽车年行驶里程（亿公里）	10.68	11.39	9.84
	公共电汽车年客运量（亿人次）	18.26	22.96	17.26
	投诉响应率（%）	100	100	100
	乘客满意率（%）	94.49	93.49	93.52
	报告期内供应商审查覆盖率（%）	100	100	100
	因社会责任不合规被否决的潜在供应商数量（个）	0	1	0
	因社会责任不合规被中止合作的供应商数量（个）	1	1	0
	供应商社会责任培训次数（次）	2	3	1

	指标	2020年	2021年	2022年
社会绩效	员工数量（人）	92264	89014	84211
	劳动合同签订率（%）	100	100	100
	社会保险覆盖率（%）	100	100	100
	女性员工比例（%）	28.33	26.49	25.43
	女性管理者比例（%）	39.34	39.30	40.54
	人均带薪年休假天数（天）	10	10	11
	员工体检覆盖率（%）	100	100	100
	员工流失率（%）	2.50	1.73	1.86
	安全生产投入（亿元）	23.30	24.08	21.64

	指标	2020年	2021年	2022年
社会绩效	安全培训覆盖率（%）	100	100	100
	安全演练覆盖率（%）	100	100	100
	交通违法率（%）	0.29	0.33	0.27
	甲方责任事故死亡率（人/百万公里）	0.00375	0.00307	0.0005
	累计志愿服务时间（万小时）	69	99	73
	困难员工帮扶资金投入（万元）	190	209	303.15
	困难员工帮扶人数（人）	989	1090	860
	疫情期间专项帮扶资金投入（万元）	858.40	-	434.22
	疫情期间专项帮扶人数（人）	8552	-	122793

	指标	2020年	2021年	2022年
环境绩效	车辆报废淘汰数量（辆）	2409	1071	1619
	碳排放量（吨）	275587	288376	246261
	二氧化碳排放量（吨）	1010484	1057378	902957
	非化石能源比重（%）	13.20	14.40	15.92
	清洁能源和新能源公交车占比（%）	87.34	91.06	94.27
	全年能源消耗总量（吨标准煤）	477415	495424	418298
	单位产值综合能耗（吨标准煤/万元）	0.25	0.24	0.20
	天然气能源使用量（万公斤）	16906	18414	15786
	电力能源使用量（万度）	46406	53208	37817
	柴油消耗量（万升）	8276	7172	2430
	年度新鲜水用水量（万立方米）	202	263	208
	氮氧化物减排量（吨）	186.25	123.41	57.05
	颗粒物减排量（吨）	0.41	0.17	0.13
	碳氢化合物减排量（吨）	40.93	80.78	30.72

指标索引

目录		CASS-CSR4.0之公共交通运输服务业	GRI Standards	页码
封面故事				P1
卷首语				P4-5
我们的问候		P2.1 P2.2 G3.1 G6.2	2-14 2 16 2-17 2-22	P6-7
走进北京公交	关于我们	P4.1 P4.3 P1.4	2-1 2-6 2-7	P8
	企业文化	P4.1 G1.1	2-6	P9
	组织机构	P4.2	2-9	P10-11
	公司治理	M1.1 M1.3 M1.4 M2.6 M3.1 M3.5 M3.6 S1.1 S1.2 S1.4	2-13 2-27 205-2	P12-15
社会责任管理	责任管理	G2.1 G2.2 G2.3 G3.1 G3.2 G3.3 G4.1	2-12 2-13	P16
	责任沟通	G6.1 G6.2 G6.3 M3.4 M3.6	2-16 2-29 3-1 3-2 3-3	P16-19
	焦点·2022	P3.1	2-16	P20-21
	责任荣誉	A3		P22-23
十年：思变求新，笃行致远		M2.1 M2.4 M2.5 M2.7 M2.12 M2.16 M3.6	201-1	P24-43
服务：民之所需行之所至	密织线网畅通城市脉动	M2.1 M2.2 M2.3	2-6	P46
	更多出行选择	M2.1 M2.4 M2.5	413-1 413-2	P47
	公交先行赋能一体化发展	M2.1 S1.4	2-24	P47-49
	数字转型，智慧出行	M2.1 M2.4 M2.5 M2.12 M3.6	2-6	P50
	每一站，与平安相伴	S3.1 S3.2 S3.3 S3.4 S3.5 S3.6	403-2 403-7 416-1 416-2	P51-56
	让你我乐享其"乘"	M2.3 M2.8 M2.9 M2.11 M2.13 M2.14 M2.15 M2.16 M2.18 M3.1	416-1	P57-59
担当：方向盘上用心坚守	冰雪映照下的冬奥保障	M2.1 M2.12 S1.4	2-6	P62-63
	护航每一次重大活动	M2.1 S1.4	2-6	P64
	同心协力抗击疫情	S4.6 S4.10	413-1	P65-67
共享：携手并进同创价值	成就每个人的价值	S2.1 S2.2 S2.3 S2.4 S2.5 S2.7 S2.8 S2.9 S2.10 S2.11 S2.13 S2.14 S2.15 S2.16 S2.17 S2.18 S2.20	2-7 2-19 401-1 401-2 403-1 403-2 403-3 403-5 403-6 403-7 404-2 405-1 407-1	P70-76
	环境友好绿色出行	E1.3 E1.6 E1.9 E1.11 E1.12 E2.1 E2.2 E2.3 E2.5 E2.6 E2.8 E2.9 E2.13 E2.15 E2.22 E2.24 E2.25 E3.1 E3.6	301-2 302-1 305-1 305-5 305-7 306-2 302-3 302-4 303-5	P77-79
	为社区留下长久感动	S4.1 S4.2 S4.3 S4.4 S4.6 S4.8 S4.10 S4.11	203-1 413-1 413-2 414-1	P80-82
	共托乡村振兴新希望	S4.5 S4.6 S4.8 S4.12 S4.13 S4.14	203-1 413-1	P83-85
未来：一路同行，向可持续		M2.1 M2.4 M2.5 M2.7 M2.12 M3.4 M3.6	2-16 203-1 302-4 413-1	P86-97
展望		M2.1 M3.6 S2.16 E1.7 A1	2-6 2-16	P98-99
关键绩效		S1.3	2-7 201-1 302-1 302-3 302-4 302-5 303-5 305-1 305-2 405-1	P100-101
指标索引		A5		P102
关于本报告		A6	2-3 2-4	P103

关于本报告

本报告是北京公共交通控股（集团）有限公司发布的第10份企业社会责任报告，旨在向各利益相关方披露公司在可持续发展方面的理念、行动和成效，促进公司与利益相关方之间的深度了解、全面沟通与良性互动，共同推进公司与社会的可持续发展。

时间范围

2022年1月1日至12月31日，为增强数据可比性、内容延续性、宣传时效性，部分内容超出上述范围。

报告变化

本报告新增了"十年：思变求新，笃行致远"章节，从十年报告发布、"重大保障、车辆、线网、场站"影像变化以及利益相关方高度关注议题领域的变革实践出发，集中展示北京公交过去十年的履责足迹。

报告范围

本报告主要披露了北京公共交通控股（集团）有限公司践行可持续发展、履行社会责任的意愿、行动和绩效。为便于表达和方便阅读，报告中，"北京公共交通控股（集团）有限公司"也以"北京公交""集团公司"和"我们"等称谓之。

数据说明

本报告中所使用数据均来自集团公司正式文件和统计报告，所引用的数据为最终统计数据。财务数据如与年度审计报告有出入，以年度审计报告为准。我们保证，本报告发布前所有数据和内容已通过集团公司管理层审核。我们承诺，本报告内容不存在任何虚假记载、误导性陈述和重大遗漏，对报告中数据的客观性和真实性负责。

参考依据

本报告编写参照国际标准化组织《ISO 26000：社会责任国际标准（2010）》、全球可持续发展标准委员会《可持续发展报告标准》（GRI Standards）、联合国《2030年可持续发展议程》、中国国家标准《社会责任报告编写指南》（GB/T 36001-2015）、中国社会科学院《中国企业社会责任报告指南4.0之公共交通运输服务业》（CASS-CSR4.0之公共交通运输服务业），兼顾中国和国际准则。

编制过程

前期准备	报告撰写	内容审核	设计发布	反馈计划
• 组建工作小组 • 同行报告对标 • 收集报告资料	• 确认报告框架 • 编制报告内容	• 审核报告内容 • 确定报告内容	• 形成报告设计 • 公开发布报告	• 收集各方反馈 • 部署下步计划

报告获取

本报告有中文和英文两种版本，均公开出版，您可通过线上购买，获取更多我们的社会责任信息。

联系地址：北京市丰台区莲花池西里 29 号
联 系 人：兰亦帆
邮政编码：100161
联系电话：0086-10-63960088

扫一扫，期待您的反馈

金钥匙·SDG领跑企业
GoldenKey·SDG Forerunner

北京公共交通控股（集团）有限公司

可持续发展是破解全球性问题的"金钥匙"。贵公司积极行动，精准识别问题症结，以创新的解决方案突破问题难点，为实现联合国2030年可持续发展目标贡献力量，入选"金钥匙·SDG领跑企业"。

Sustainable development is the "golden key" to solve global problems. The company has been selected as "Golden Key·SDG Forerunner" for its proactive actions to accurately identify the problems and provide with innovative solutions to contribute to the achievement of the UN 2030 Sustainable Development Goals.

可持续发展 经济导刊
CHINA SUSTAINABILITY TRIBUNE

图书在版编目（CIP）数据

北京公交社会责任报告 . 2022/北京公共交通控股（集团）有限公司编著 . —北京：经济管理出版社，2023. 10

ISBN 978-7-5096-9418-3

Ⅰ . ①北 … Ⅱ . ①北… Ⅲ . ①公交公司—企业责任—研究报告—北京—2022 Ⅳ . ①F512. 71

中国国家版本馆 CIP 数据核字（2023）第 213988 号

责任编辑：张莉琼
责任印制：黄章平

出版发行：经济管理出版社
　　　　　（北京市海淀区北蜂窝 8 号中雅大厦 A 座 11 层　100038）
网　　址：www. E-mp. com. cn
电　　话：（010）51915602
印　　刷：唐山玺诚印务有限公司
经　　销：新华书店
开　　本：889mm×1194mm/16
印　　张：13. 5
字　　数：382 千字
版　　次：2023 年 12 月第 1 版　2023 年 12 月第 1 次印刷
书　　号：ISBN 978-7-5096-9418-3
定　　价：138. 00 元（全二册）

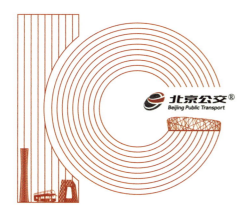

Time is silent, yet leaves its footprint. Beijing Public Transport Corporation (BPTC), under the strong leadership of the CPC, has forged ahead in the new era and pursued development through reform and innovation. 2022 marks the tenth year since the first social responsibility report of BPTC was issued. In the past decade, BPTC has progressed in tandem with the capital in a glorious and full-of-expectations journey. Our buses travel across the city day in and day out, offering quality mobility services to people and bearing witness to the changes in Beijing. Our buses run for passengers and our bus route network covers the city. As a responsible corporation, BPTC will be committed to a denser bus route network and a more intensive use of public transport infrastructures, driving towards a better future of sustainable development.

CSR Management Committee of BPTC

Directors

Zhu Kai

Deputy Directors

Sha Yong	Gao Yurong	Gao Ming	Wang Xiuying	Chang Jiang
Chen Wancheng	Geng Zhencheng	Cui Di	Hong Chongyue	Ji Langchao
Cao Yan	Zou Yanhuan	Meng Hong	Han Congbi	

Committee Members

Xu Zhengxiang	Zhang Zeying	Liu Huizhong	Gao yuan	Kong Weifeng
Zhao Chao	Wan Yifei	Xu Liquan	Yang Bin	Shao Qiang
Zhou Jianyong	Tian Guihong	Shao Dan	Wang Yongjie	Jiang Huamao
Zhang Zheng	Nan Ziye	Zhang Bin		

CSR Reporting Preparation Committee of BPTC

Chief editor

Xu Zhengxiang

Deputy editors in chief

Hu Liwen	Han Yunzhe	Pu Xiaomin

Members

Lan Yifan	Feng Shuai	Li Jingya	Ji Peilong	Che Xun
Zhao Ying	Zhao Liuyin	Zhao Yipu	Zheng Ying	Li Beini
Geng Zihou	Liu Tongzheng	Zhang Fushun	Zhang Jie	Yu Jiayuan
Tang Wenlan	Wang Chao (Operational Dispatch Control Center)		Liu Xiang	Hu Jie
Yao Yuan	Fan Siqi	Cui Qingde	Chen Xiaojun	Tian Qingxia
Han Dexia	Lu Gege	Sun Dandan		

Photography

Wang Chao (Publicity Department)	Li Tianci	Zhang Xuan

Proofreading

Li Jingya	Lan Yifan	Liu Tongzheng

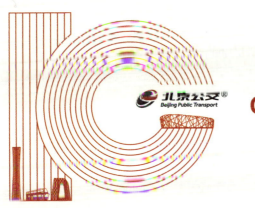

CONTENTS

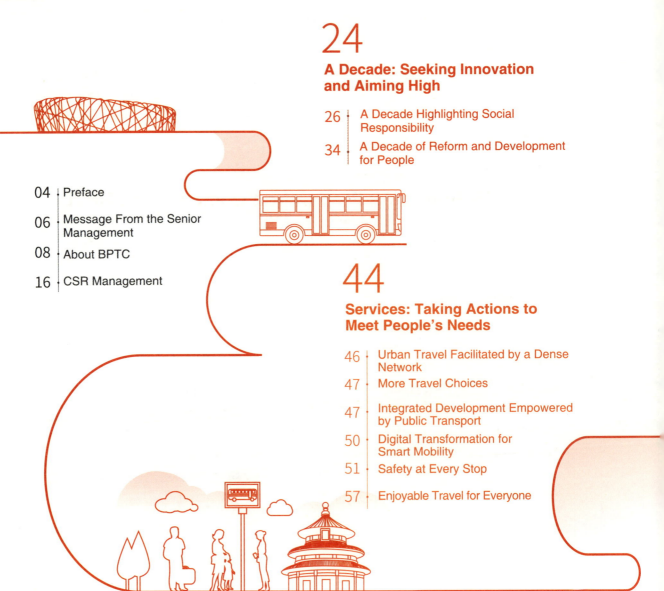

24

A Decade: Seeking Innovation and Aiming High

26 | A Decade Highlighting Social Responsibility

34 | A Decade of Reform and Development for People

04 | Preface

06 | Message From the Senior Management

08 | About BPTC

16 | CSR Management

44

Services: Taking Actions to Meet People's Needs

46 | Urban Travel Facilitated by a Dense Network

47 | More Travel Choices

47 | Integrated Development Empowered by Public Transport

50 | Digital Transformation for Smart Mobility

51 | Safety at Every Stop

57 | Enjoyable Travel for Everyone

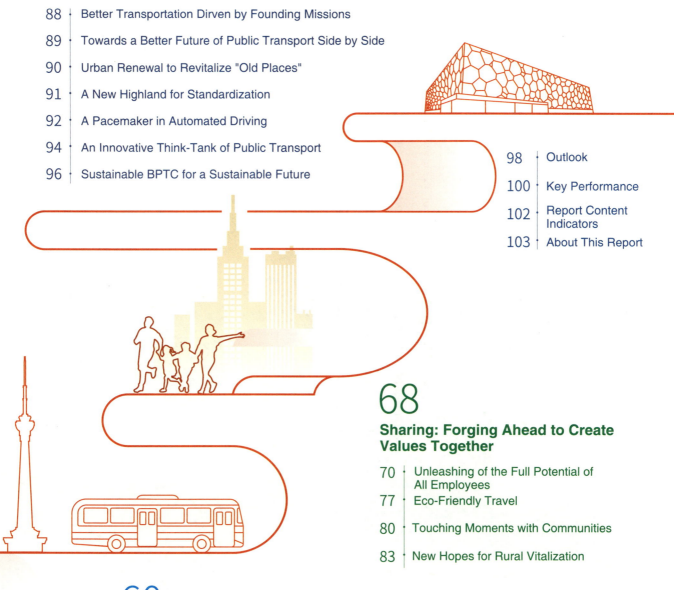

86

Prospect: Accompanying You All the Way Towards a Sustainable Future

88 ┊ Better Transportation Dirven by Founding Missions

89 ┊ Towards a Better Future of Public Transport Side by Side

90 ┊ Urban Renewal to Revitalize "Old Places"

91 ┊ A New Highland for Standardization

92 ┊ A Pacemaker in Automated Driving

94 ┊ An Innovative Think-Tank of Public Transport

96 ┊ Sustainable BPTC for a Sustainable Future

98 ┊ Outlook

100 ┊ Key Performance

102 ┊ Report Content Indicators

103 ┊ About This Report

68

Sharing: Forging Ahead to Create Values Together

70 ┊ Unleashing of the Full Potential of All Employees

77 ┊ Eco-Friendly Travel

80 ┊ Touching Moments with Communities

83 ┊ New Hopes for Rural Vitalization

60

Responsibility: Dedicating Ourselves to Bus Operations

62 ┊ Transport Services for the Beijing 2022 Olympic Winter Games

64 ┊ Transport Services for Major Events

65 ┊ Joint Fight Against COVID-19

In a decade of endeavor with green development as the fundamental feature

Eco-friendly buses cultivated a new trend of clean travel

In a decade of endeavor with a commitment to sharing benefits

A new pattern of urban-rural equalized access to services and regional integrated development has been explored

Looking back and forward

A grand blueprint is gradually unfolding

On a new journey

BPTC will be more steadfast

We will optimize services to keep up with passengers' needs

We will explore the new value of public transport to answer the call of our times

We will advance innovation-driven development through empowerment of intelligent technology

We will take a lead in building an industrial ecology to strengthen the industry

We will engage with stakeholders to build a community of development

Hand in hand, we press ahead

For more passenger-friendly, convenient, expedite, flexible, and diverse public transport

For a better and more sustainable future together

Transport connects the world and great paths point to the future

BPTC is with you all the time

Preface

It's another day after the moon has set

It's another spring after the winter has gone

BPTC lived up to its responsibility

With buses navigating through the entire city

And employees withstanding major tests

Each bus running on the road and each mile covered

Witness the change in transportation, the city, and even the times

Attesting to BPTC's mission to deliver better public transport services to more people

In a decade of endeavor with the people's expectations as our original aspirations

We offered high-quality and diversified bus services to the satisfaction of passengers

In a decade of endeavor with responsibility taken seriously

We delivered exceptional transport services for major events

In a decade of endeavor with innovation as the engine

Digitalization has fostered new drivers of high-quality development

Message From the Senior Management

The last decade has been arduously fruitful.

In 2013, Chinese President, Xi Jinping, pointed out that "developing public transport is the direction of developing modern cities". In response, the CPC Central Committee and the State Council respectively issued the *Outline for Building a Country with Strong Transportation Network and the National Comprehensive Three-dimensional Transportation Network Planning Outline*, which highlight the priority of urban public transport and the further implementation of "public transport first" strategy, pointing out the direction for the development of public transport. In the "14th Five-Year Plan" period (2021-2025), the CPC Beijing Municipal Committee and Beijing Municipal People's Government, assign a new role and new requirements to BPTC – "building a modern comprehensive service provider of urban public transport" that coordinates the two main business sectors of comprehensive urban passenger transport service and automobile service and trade.

In the past decade, guided by Xi Jinping Thought on Socialism with Chinese Characteristics for a New Era and under the strong leadership of the CPC Beijing Municipal Committee and Beijing Municipal People's Government, we have forged ahead as one and met the tasks and targets of ten-year in-depth reform on all fronts, thus improving our corporate governance system and modernizing our governance capacity. Ten years on, we have regarded innovation as the primary driver of development by placing it at the core of the overall corporate development and continued to bring out new ideas, models, and services, transforming ground public transport to be passenger-oriented, personalized, digitalized, and intelligent. The past decade has witnessed our efforts to put passengers first, empower stakeholders, and fulfill CSR, with the release of social responsibility reports for ten consecutive years. All these endeavors make up a remarkable chapter of BPTC as a responsible ground public transport service provider in the capital of a big country.

Moments offer a glimpse into our past decade. We unswervingly follow the Party line, serve the Party's mission, and deliver the Party's orders. Keeping in mind the responsibility of an SOE, we decisively make our contribution to major political tasks. For example, we offered transport services for the celebration of the 70th anniversary of the founding of the People's Republic of China, the 100th anniversary of the founding of the Communist Party of China, and the Beijing 2022 Winter Olympics and Paralympics (Beijing 2022). As we ushered in BPTC's 100th anniversary in 2021, we reviewed and paid tribute to our glorious past by compiling *Centenary BPTC* and producing 100 micro-videos on the development of BPTC. We also successfully held the 100th-anniversary ceremony presenting different performances to pass on the Corporation's legacy for a new journey to come. Struck by the sudden outbreak of COVID-19, we put people and life first, made careful deployment and science-based prevention and control, carried out nucleic acid tests for all employees, regularly disinfected all operating vehicles and stations, and implemented temporary operation control measures such as stop-skipping and short-turnning operation. These measures helped us pull through challenges together and ensured the safe and orderly operation of ground public transport in the capital.

We pursue innovation and offer sincere services. Committed to the corporate mission of "delivering better public transport services to more people", we have optimized the bus network thoroughly, promoted digital transformation, and vigorously established regional intelligent operation control centers. We also continue to explore new business models and serve the coordinated development of the Beijing-Tianjin-Hebei region to meet the needs of people for better transport services. In 2022, exclusive bus lanes in the capital increased to 1,005 lane kilometers, and a network of bus lanes in the Beijing-Kaiyuan Expressway, the Third Ring Road, the Beijing-Lhasa Expressway, and the Beijing–Hong Kong–Macau Expressway took shape. The length of the conventional bus routes of BPTC has risen to 30,173.9 kilometers, with nearly 200 corridor bus routes in a layout of "chessboard + ring + radiation". Through intelligent operation control, the adherence rate of bus schedules has been over 99% and the departure punctuality rate exceeded 98%. There have been 418 customized bus routes, saving more than 30% of commute time. The total length of bus routes in Xiong'an New Area amounted to 347.1 kilometers, which helped deepen the Beijing-Tianjin-Hebei coordinated development.

We prioritize the environment and green development. Deeply understanding and following the principle that "lucid waters and lush mountains are invaluable assets" proposed by Chinese President Xi Jinping, we have taken action to serve China's 30•60 Decarbonization Goal (China strives to peak carbon dioxide emissions by 2030 and achieve carbon neutrality by 2060), complied with the corresponding "1+N" policy system, and promoted green and low-carbon development. We decommissioned old buses at a faster pace, updated green and low-carbon equipment, and built more supporting facilities such as charging piles, hydrogen refueling stations, and intelligent electronic stop signs. In 2022, BPTC's clean energy and new energy buses accounted for 94.27% of the fleet, and the construction of two hydrogen refueling stations and 1,524 charging piles in 225 bus depots was completed. In 2022, BPTC's carbon emissions trading totaled 114,100 tons, bringing in a net income of RMB 11,650,200.

We dare to break into uncharted territories. Deeply aware that "innovation is the primary driving force behind development", we took an innovation-oriented approach and explored emerging fields with an enterprising spirit, setting precedents in different aspects of the public transport industry. We put forward the new concept of "Mobility as Life", so that public transport serves as a means of transport and a mobile life setting that offers a new blueprint of "urban mobile living room". Focusing on cutting-edge autonomous driving technology and the strategic development of future intelligent transport, we cooperated with Toyota to pilot self-driving bus operation in Shougang Park and with BAIC Foton and other industry-university-research organizations to carry out self-driving bus demonstration projects. We also set up the first postdoctoral research center in China's public transport industry, which introduced the first group of postdoctoral researchers, aimed to build a new-type public transport think tank with a global vision and competitiveness. These efforts will accelerate BPTC's transformation from a labor-intensive to a high-tech-intensive enterprise.

We stand together through thick and thin and strive for a shared future. Working closely with stakeholders, we have been benefited from co-created development results. Under the strategy of making a talent-strong BPTC, we took multiple measures to promote employee vocational education and talent training to unleash everyone's potential. Meanwhile, we continue to strengthen elderly-oriented renovations and improve barrier-free travel services. In 2022, BPTC put in place more than 14,000 low-floor vehicles, including more than 12,000 vehicles with wheelchair ramps, and urban buses with accessible facilities made up 80%. We helped Hebei, Inner Mongolia, Tibet, Xinjiang, Hubei, and other areas consolidate and expand the achievements of poverty alleviation and ensure an effective transition to rural vitalization. We assisted people in Nangou Village of Beijing Miyun District to increase their incomes and helped the three villages with a weak collective economy in Mentougou District shore up their weaknesses. We also improved the coverage of bus routes in mountainous areas and guaranteed public transport services to every village to promote rural vitalization on all fronts. We worked together with multiple cities around the world to transform the consensus of the *Declaration on Building a Community for Public Transport Development* into profound practice. The Declaration depicts a vision to build a closely linked community on public transport development and develop public transport systems that are more human-oriented, convenient and expedited, comfortable and safe, energy-saving and eco-friendly, flexible and diversified.

Emerging from self-transformation in the last decade, we set sail toward the next chapter. The year 2023 marks the first year of fully implementing the guiding principles of the 20th CPC National Congress and a crucial junction in the 14th Five-Year Plan period (2021-2025). Building on the last decade of strengths, BPTC will serve the development goals of the 14th Five-Year Plan and the long-range objectives through the year 2035, move forward with courage and perseverance, and strive to build a domestically leading and world-class modern comprehensive service provider of urban public transport, with an aim to improve passengers' sense of gain, happiness, and security.

About BPTC

Corporate Profile

Beijing Public Transport Corporation (BPTC) is a large-scale wholly state-owned public transport enterprise group. Based on the operation of ground public transport and supported by diversified investment methods and types of economies, the Corporation integrates services of passenger transport, vehicle repair, tourism, vehicle rental, advertising, etc. According to BPTC's 14th Five-Year Plan, the Corporation has established two main business sectors, namely, comprehensive urban passenger transport service and automobile service and trade. With the capital as the foothold, we serve the Beijing-Tianjin-Hebei region and strive to build a domestically leading and world class modern comprehensive service provider of urban public transport.

We play a principal role in Beijing's ground public transport and are key to the development of Beijing's urban public transport system. By the end of 2022, we had total assets of RMB 64.327 billion, net assets of RMB 44.44 billion, and 84,211 employees. We operated with a fleet of 32,783 vehicles, among which 23,465 were buses and trolleybuses, with the proportion of clean energy and new energy vehicles reaching 94.27%. We operated 1,291 scheduled bus routes, 418 customized bus routes, and 158 routes for flexible services. In 2022, we covered a distance of 984 million kilometers, with 1.726 billion annual passenger trips. At the same time, we operate two modern tram lines-Xijiao Line and ETOWN T1 Line.

Comprehensive urban passenger transport service ···········

Automobile service and trade

Two primary businesses

Including bus and trolleybus services, bus tourism, advertising and media, investment, financing and asset management around passenger transport

Including driving training, automobile sales, automobile leasing, automobile repair, and the dismantling and recycling of expired automobiles

Companionship Culture

Mission
Deliver better public transport services
to more people

Vision
Lead the way for the public to travel, raise the quality
of city life, and build a world-renowned modern comprehensive service group for urban public transport

Core value
Put people first   Give utmost care to passengers
Promote innovation   Pursue excellence

BPTC spirit
Serve passengers heart and soul
Take pride in providing services
Contribute sincerely to society
Take responsibility with courage

Organization structure

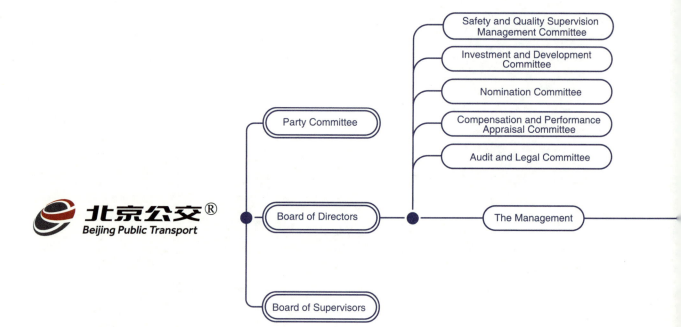

First Passenger Transport Branch

Second Passenger Transport Branch

Third Passenger Transport Branch

Fourth Passenger Transport Branch

Fifth Passenger Transport Branch

Sixth Passenger Transport Branch

Seventh Passenger Transport Branch

Eighth Passenger Transport Branch

Ninth Passenger Transport Branch

Trolley Bus Branch

Maintenance and Repair Branch

Hongyuncheng Property Management Centre

Asset Management Branch

Site/Station Management Branch

Party Committee Office
(Inspection Section, Supervision Center
Customer Service Center)

Strategy, Reform and Development Department

Legal Department

Finance Department
(Treasury Management Center)

Audit Department (Audit Center)

Human Resources Department

Asset Management Center

Capital Operation Center

Network Center

Operational Dispatch Control Center

Safety and Service Department

Science and Technology Information Department (Data Center)

Security Department (Emergency Management Center)

Infrastructure and Administration Department

Organization Department

Publicity Department
(Corporate Culture Center)

Discipline and Supervision Office

Labour Union

Communist Youth League Committee

Beijing Bus Media Co., Ltd.

Beijing Beiqi Taxi Group Co., Ltd.

Beijing Bus Guang'an Business Trade Group

Beijing Public Transport Corporation Asset Management Co., Ltd.

Beijing Public Transport Tram Corporation

Beijing Gongjiao Driving School Co.,Ltd.

Beijing Public Transport Group Asset Management Laishui Co., Ltd.

Beijing Public Transport Group Urban Renewal Operation and Management Co., Ltd.

Beijing Public Transport Group Party School

Beijing Public Transport Senior Technical School

Corporate Governance

BPTC, firmly upholding the Party leadership, promotes the modernization of governance system and capability, continuously optimizes the corporate governance system, and strengthens awareness of systems and standards. While adhering to law-based governance, compliance management and integrity operation, BPTC enhances risk management and control in an all-round manner to ensure sustainable and sound corporate development.

Party leadership

Watching the grand opening ceremony of the 20th CPC National Congress

Bearing in mind the political duties of state-owend enterprises, BPTC comprehensively promotes the deep integration of Party building with business operations. In the year of convening the 20th CPC National Congress, we carried out company-wide in-depth study activities in a comprehensive, multi-tiered, and multifaceted way, initiated various publicity campaigns that conform to the times, followed the law of development and display great creativity, and guided Party members to study more actively and aim for higher goals in thorough understanding and effective implementation. In this way, we keep intensifying our study efforts to inspire the powerful spiritual strength for forging ahead on a new journey and making contributions to the new era.

"All of us in the Party must bear in mind that full and rigorous self-governance is an unceasing endeavor and that self-reform is a journey to which there is no end." We resolutely uphold General Secretary Xi Jinping's status as the core of the CPC Central Committee and the whole Party, as well as the authority and centralized, unified leadership of the CPC Central Committee, and enhance political oversight by focusing on transport missions for the Beijing 2022 Olympic Winter Games and the 20th CPC National Congress. We foster positive atmosphere to tackle pointless formalities, bureaucratism, hedonism, and extravagance, and work tirelessly to implement the Party's eight-point frugality code, with the aim to win the tough and protracted battle of improving Party conduct. Prioritizing the tightening of Party discipline, we have taken coordinated steps to ensure that officials do not have the audacity, opportunity, or desire to be corrupt, steadily fostering a sound political ecosystem featuring honesty and integrity. We make full use of the "Clean BPTC" and Integrity Education Base as the platforms to carry out anti-corruption awareness education and publicity on Party conduct and clean governance, bolstering CPC members and cadres' ideological and moral defense line against corruption and moral decline.

28

Meetings of the Standing Committee of the Party Committee

227

Issues studied

13,413

Party members

375

Party branches

4,212

Party-building activities

693

Hours of training on Party building

Group-wide publicity lectures on studying, publicizing, and implementing the guiding principles of the 20th CPC National Congress

The Fourth CPC Congress of BPTC

Governance mechanism

BPTC has resolutely implemented the decision-making system of "decisions on a major event, appointment and removal of important officials, important project arrangements, and use of large amounts of funds", strictly followed the "top-of-the-agenda" system (making the learning of Xi Jinping Thought on Socialism with Chinese Characteristics for a New Era, Xi's important speeches and the Party Constitution and major policies top of the agenda of Party meetings at all levels) of the Corporation, and formulated the *Board Authorized Decision-making Plan and Authorization List* to clarify relevant rules of procedure. At the same time, we guided all secondary subsidiaries to perfect the "one brochure for one enterprise" filing process, gradually improve corporate governance, and enhance the modernization of governance system and capability.

7

Board Meetings

61

Issues discussed by the Board

63

Issues discussed by specialized committees

26

Meetings of Management Office

221

Issues discussed by the Management Office

Deeper SOE reform

BPTC has thoroughly implemented the three-year action plan for SOE reform. Focusing on the development of the whole process of public transport, the whole industry chain, and the whole lifecycle of corporate development, we have gradually improved the allocation of human, financial and material resources within the Corporation, optimized business layout, and promoted cost reduction and efficiency improvement through systematic planning. After deepening reforms in all aspects and across all levels, we have accomplished 99 key reform tasks in 6 aspects with high-quality, which promoted the high-quality corporate development and thus empowered BPTC with new vitality, making impressive achievements in the SOE reform. As a result, BPTC was rated excellent in the 2021 assessment of the three-year action for SOE reform by the State-owned Assets Supervision and Administration Commission of People's Government of Beijing Municipality and the video about BPTC's implementation of the three-year action of SOE reform was released on the official website of the State-owned Assets Supervision and Administration Commission of the State Council (SASAC).

Scan the QR code to watch the promo of *Unswervingly Deepening Reform Across the Board and Striving to Build the Public Transport Industry of a Big Country – BPTC's Record of Implementing the Three-Year Action Plan for SOE Reform*

33
Subsidiaries establish the Board of Directors that is legally required

100%
Achieved a majority of external directors in the Board

51
Subsidiaries

Completed the tenure system and contract-based management among senior managers

100%
Coverage rate

131
Signatories in total

Law-based corporate governance

Bearing in mind the principle of "believing in the rule of law, and realizing law-based decision-making and reform, compliance management and operation", BPTC has implemented overall law-based corporate governance to effectively prevent compliance risks. In 2022, we held the compliance management system development and deployment meeting, formulated and issued the *Implementation Plan of Building the Compliance Management System*, and promoted a compliance management system with full participation, whole-process monitoring and company-wide coverage in accordance with the four-step strategy of "deployment and preparation, pilot implementation, comprehensive application, summary and improvement". Adhering to process control, we took the initiative to carry out special ratification for internal control, continuously improve intellectual property management, and vigorously advanced standardization. We successfully completed the three-year standardization action, passed the final assessment and acceptance of national standardization pilot projects with high scores. The revised Beijing local standard, *General Technical Specifications for Bus*, which BPTC took the lead in the process, was officially approved and released.

The meeting of compliance management system development and deployment

National Constitution Day and Rule of Law Publicity Week activities

The three-year standardization action plan review and awards ceremony

Audit supervision

BPTC optimizes the audit mode, methods and processes, and promotes the transformation of audit to whole-process supervision of all stages, before, during and after an incident. Focusing on the implementation of major decisions, the management and control of key areas, use of large sum of funds, we have formulated and implemented the "three-year full coverage" work plan for the supervision and evaluation of internal control of subsidiaries of the Corporation to ensure the compliance and effectiveness of key projects and capital investment of our subsidiaries through targeted and effective implementation across the board. At the same time, we have strengthened publicity and education on auditing policies and regulations, compiled and published 4 digital special issues and 43 issues of updates on audit, creating a sound cultural environment for audit. In 2022, 76 audit projects and 165 audit tasks in total were completed, with an annual rectification rate of 99.1%, providing strong support for SOE reform and high-quality development.

27
Corporate standards released

28
Issues of Rule of Law Highlights published

67
Issues of Current Events on Rule of Law published

72
Articles on the Corporate Wechat Column Law-based Public Transport published

By the end of 2022,

8
Patents for inventions obtained in total

60
Utility patents obtained in total

CSR Management

Serving wholeheartedly, BPTC proactively takes on its responsibility and holds its position as a company dedicated to public welfare. With clear CSR awareness and concrete actions, we incorporate CSR philosophy into our development strategy, corporate management, and daily operations so that our core advantages can be leveraged to facilitate the coordinated development of the economy, environment, and society. We have established an effective CSR management system to promote communication among stakeholders and provide long-term momentum for our operation.

Management Approach

BPTC highly values CSR management and assigns work based on a CSR management structure with well-defined authority and responsibility and orderly operations. To further improve CSR management system, we have formed a stable, well-structured, and efficient CSR management team consisting of CSR editors across the business lines and reporters of our secondary subsidiaries. Meanwhile, we gradually standardize the work process, including CSR report preparation, review, release, promotion, as well as communication and interviews with stakeholders, to improve the efficiency and quality of our CSR management.

CSR Communication

Listening to the voices of various groups is the first step of BPTC's CSR fulfillment. With a deep understanding of our social responsibility, we develop our reports into a platform and media for stakeholder communication through surveys on material topics, Transport Open Day, public transport fans meetings, etc. Built on it, we strive to establish and show an image as a responsible, respected, and sustainable company.

Material topics

With deep analysis of domestic and international CSR standards and the macro environment of sustainable development, we benchmark industry players with excellent CSR performance, combine our development strategy in the new era and our planning set for the 14th Five-Year Plan period (2021-2025), and comply with principles of focusing on material topics, presenting complete information and engaging with stakeholders. Accordingly, we prioritize material topics and draw a materiality matrix from two dimensions, "Significance to economic, environmental and social impacts" and "Impact on stakeholder assessment & decisions". This approach makes the report present the contribution from internal and external groups, and also provides a reference for the CSR reporting preparation and work progress.

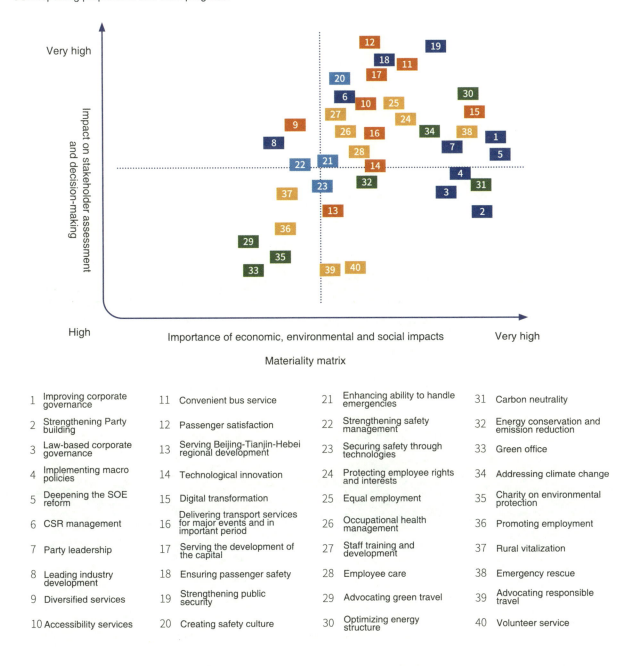

Materiality matrix

1 Improving corporate governance	11 Convenient bus service	21 Enhancing ability to handle emergencies	31 Carbon neutrality
2 Strengthening Party building	12 Passenger satisfaction	22 Strengthening safety management	32 Energy conservation and emission reduction
3 Law-based corporate governance	13 Serving Beijing-Tianjin-Hebei regional development	23 Securing safety through technologies	33 Green office
4 Implementing macro policies	14 Technological innovation	24 Protecting employee rights and interests	34 Addressing climate change
5 Deepening the SOE reform	15 Digital transformation	25 Equal employment	35 Charity on environmental protection
6 CSR management	16 Delivering transport services for major events and in important period	26 Occupational health management	36 Promoting employment
7 Party leadership	17 Serving the development of the capital	27 Staff training and development	37 Rural vitalization
8 Leading industry development	18 Ensuring passenger safety	28 Employee care	38 Emergency rescue
9 Diversified services	19 Strengthening public security	29 Advocating green travel	39 Advocating responsible travel
10 Accessibility services	20 Creating safety culture	30 Optimizing energy structure	40 Volunteer service

Note: In the review of CSR topics in 2022, based on the CSR development trend and current hotspots at home and abroad, we raised the prioritization of the topic 5 "Deepening the SOE reform" and the topic 15 "Digital transformation".

Stakeholder communication

Communication activities have been carried out in various forms and with diverse contents. Through multiple platforms, we further understand and actively respond to the expectations and demands of all stakeholders on our sustainable development, together with more groups for a better future of travel.

Stakeholders	Expectations and appeals	Responses
The government	Complying with laws and regulations Implementing transportation plans of the government Serving regional economic development Increasing employment Response to COVID-19 prevention and control requirements	Compliance management and risk control Paying tax Accepting the supervision of the government proactively Serving Beijing-Tianjin-Hebei integrated development Undertaking COVID-19 prevention and control measures on a regular basis
Passengers	Quality and considerate services Ensuring safe travel	Providing diversified travel services Promoting accessibility Passenger satisfaction survey Handling of customer complaints Driving safety training Safety and emergency management
Employees	Basic rights and interests Employee development Employee care	Improving compensation and benefit system Labor unions and worker representative congress Occupational health and safety management Launching staff trainings Assisting needy employees
The industry / partners	Abiding by business ethics Promoting shared development among the industry	Responsible purchasing Combating unfair competition Promoting technological innovation Conducting strategic cooperation with partners Actively supporting the work of industrial associations
Communities	Enhancing community co-construction Contributing to public welfare	Providing volunteer service Facilitating rural vitalization Promoting social employment Advocating responsible travel
The environment	Abiding by environmental laws and regulations Environmental protection	Conserving energy and reducing emissions Promoting new energy vehicles Waste sorting and Clean Your Plate Campaign Advocating green travel Public welfare activities on afforestation

BPTC held the opening ceremony of *Centenary BPTC*.

BPTC carried out an activity of "Forging Ahead on a New Journey and striving for New Changes in Public Transport & 2023 Visit of BPTC by Social Media Influencers".

The Seventh Passenger Transport Branch organized the Safety Month campaign.

T116 buses were themed Grand Canal Culture.

Highlights in 2022

January

We launched the innovative offering "superior buses" that adopted the operation mode of "fixed routes and stations, planned schedules, and on-demand dispatch", allowing passengers to book online for services in groups.

The personnel and vehicles got ready at the Beijing and Yanqing competition zones of the Beijing 2022 Olympic Winter Games and started transport services from January 21 inside the Olympic bubble.

February

The Party Committee and the governing body of BPTC jointly issued the *Outline of the Development Plan Set for the 14th Five-Year Plan Period and Long-Range Objectives Through the Year 2035*.

The new energy training base of AUV buses of the Beijing Public Transport Senior Technical School was completed.

We released the *Three-Year Plan for Building an Industry-Education-Integrated Enterprise (2021-2023)*.

March

We accomplished the task of guaranteeing transport services for the "two sessions", namely the annual sessions of the National People's Congress and the National Committee of the Chinese People's Political Consultative Conference.

We provided transport services for the Beijing 2022 and received more than 80 thank-you letters and hanging pennants from the Beijing Organising Committee for the 2022 Olympic and Paralympic Winter Games, the Norwegian Olympic and Paralympic Committee and Confederation of Sports, the General Administration of Sport of China, the Yanqing District Government, and the venue hotels.

We cooperated with Toyota to pilot self-driving bus operations in Shougang Park, a competition venue of the Beijing 2022.

August

BPTC issued the *Work Plan for Building a New System of Modern Traffic Safety Management*.

We released the "Accompany You All the Way" bus travel service application.

Beijing Public Transport Tram Corporation set up a "summer open day" on the Xijiao Line, inviting more than 40 primary and secondary students to have a field trip to learn about the daily operation and the history of trams.

We revised the *Provisions on the Administration of Labor Contracts*.

September

We accomplished the transport services for the 2022 China International Fair for Trade in Services.

We launched the customized bus service of "to-school service", and employed the customized bus application and WeChat mini program platform to establish a communication mechanism with schools and parents and collect the needs for transport services to schools.

Ding Yanxin, Deputy Director General of the Safety and Quality Supervision and Management Department of the Ministry of Transport, led an inspection team to the BPTC to inspect the preparations for major activities and offer guidance on work safety.

We held the 2022 Driver "Gold and Silver Steering Wheel Award" ceremony.

We adjusted Route T105 and Route 317 to the Zhangjiawan Design Town to facilitate the travel of people in the town.

October

We signed a strategic cooperation agreement with the Beijing Postal Branch of China Post Group Corporation Limited to jointly explore a new mechanism of "bus-postal cooperation".

The launch ceremony of the *Centenary BPTC* was held.

The first group of postdoctoral researchers entered the postdoctoral research center of BPTC.

We met the annual carbon emission compliance and emission control responsibilities.

We organized Party members and employees to watch the opening ceremony of the 20th National Congress of the CPC live through TV, internet, and radio to get the message of solidarity and greater efforts in this era.

April

We were awarded the title of "Outstanding Contribution Collective for Beijing 2022 Winter Olympics and Paralympics" by the CPC Central Committee and the State Council.

The Baiyangdian Wharf and surrounding road and landscape improvement project completed project acceptance.

Israeli ambassador to China Irit Ben-Abba led a delegation to visit BPTC, hoping to further strengthen exchanges and cooperation in the sci-tech industry to benefit the two peoples.

May

We signed a strategic cooperation agreement with the Beijing Academy of Blockchain and Edge Computing to shape a new pattern of digital public transport and create a "Beijing model" for the digital transformation of the public transport industry.

The VIP fleet of business branch under Beijing Beiqi Taxi Group Co., Ltd. offered the transport service when President Xi Jinping met with John Lee, the sixth-term chief executive of the Hong Kong Special Administrative Region.

In response to the roads opened to traffic around Fengtai Railway Station and the completion of the temporary bus stop of the station, we launched the special Route 149 and adjusted the special Route 4 to offer transfer services for the station.

July

BPTC issued and implemented the *Work Measures on Supporting the Development of Customized Bus Services* to promote the rapid development of customized bus services.

More than 9,300 buses engaged in the publicity of non-profit activities to foster a friendly atmosphere of whole-of-society care for new entrants into the workforce.

We strengthened communication and cooperation with cultural advancement centers at the municipal and district levels and encouraged all subsidiaries to visit or hold exchange activities for bus stop guides.

To improve passenger satisfaction and operational efficiency, we shortened the first and last three trips of the 12 trains of the ETOWN T1 Line from 49 minutes to 45 minutes.

Ji Xinrong, a senior deputy manager, was selected as one of the 10th group of cadres in Beijing to assist Tibet in a three-year targeted support program for Tibet.

June

We undertook 70 bus routes in Tongzhou and assigned the BPTC Urban Sub-Center Passenger Transport Co., Ltd. to take charge of the operation of regional bus routes covering an area of 906 square kilometers in Tongzhou.

We donated COVID-19 preventive materials worth about RMB 10,000 to three economically weak villages which received our targeted assistance, namely Facheng, Gaopu, and Huanglingxi, in Zhaitang Town of Mentougou District.

Wei Xiaodong, Secretary of the Beijing CPPCC Party Group and Chairman, led a team to visit BPTC for a "one group for one enterprise" inspection.

Buses synchronize the function of QR code scanning for ticketing and COVID-19 health check.

We issued and implemented the *Overall Plan for Deepening the Reform of the Maintenance System in the New Era*.

We implemented the requirements of facilitating the application of Beijing central axis for the title of World Heritage Site, moving Route 110 out of Tianqiao Bus Station.

November

We launched customized bus services in Lize Financial Business District.

We passed the final evaluation of the national social management and public service comprehensive standardization pilot project with a high score.

In the national finals of the 4th Micro Lesson Competition, we took home all the top ten prizes and won 20 individual awards. Wang Qinghui from the Eighth Passenger Transport Branch appeared on the stage of the Jinke Award PK Competition.

We launched Route 502 and adjusted Route 396 to facilitate passengers in Sanjiadian and Wulituo to quickly connect to Metro Line 6 through Shiguang Road Expressway.

December

The revised Beijing local standard, *General Technical Specifications for Bus* (DB11/T 532-2022), which BPTC took the lead in the process, was approved and released by the Beijing Municipal Administration for Market Regulation.

We launched five urban and rural bus routes in Rongcheng County in Xiong'an New Area, namely Routes 361, 362, 363, 365, and 367.

BPTC issued the *Themed Route Construction Plan*.

The newly opened cross-regional peripheral general route, Route 903, has become the key route from Fangshan District directly to Mentougou District with the highest single-day passenger trips of over 10,000.

The construction of the main bus terminal in the west of the cultural and tourism zone in Tongzhou District was completed, the Huilongguan bus maintenance yard and bus depot project was completed, and the main structure of the Fushouling Main Bus Terminal was completed.

We signed cooperation agreements for the first 11 targets of the bus retail service project, and the first mobile dining bus was put into operation at the Chongwenmen Route 111 bus depot.

The three-year action of SOE reform was successfully concluded, and 99 key reform tasks in six aspects were completed remarkably.

CSR Honors

Our collective honors and accolades (partial)

BPTC was awarded the "Outstanding Contribution Collective for Beijing 2022 Winter Olympics and Paralympics" by the CPC Central Committee and the State Council.

BPTC received the "2022 National Safety Culture Building Demonstration Enterprise" from China Association of Work Safety.

BPTC won the second prize of Energy Conservation and Emission Reduction Technology Progress Award by the China Energy Conservation Association.

The case of "BPTC key technology application for digital operation" received the first prize of "Dingxin Cup" digital transformation and industry integration at the 2022 Digital Transformation Summit Forum jointly hosted by the China Academy of Information and Communications Technology and the China Association of Communication Enterprises.

The "Accompany You" cultural brand of BPTC was granted the first prize of model cultural brands in the national transportation industry.

BPTC's project won the first prize of the 36th Beijing Innovation Achievement in Corporate Management Modernization.

BPTC was recognized with the title of "municipal traffic safety excellent system" in 2022 presented by the Beijing municipal traffic safety department joint conference.

BPTC won the title of "2022 Beijing Copyright Protection Model" by the Publicity Department of the CPC Beijing Municipal Committee.

BPTC got the title of "Beijing Advanced Group for Energy Conservation and Emission Reduction" jointly presented by the Beijing Municipal Commission of Development and Reform and Beijing Municipal Ecology and Environment Bureau.

BPTC's 100th-anniversary theme song *Centennial BPTC* was released and awarded the first prize of the Beijing professional news award by the Beijing Journalism Society.

BPTC and Beijing Beiqi Taxi Group Co., Ltd. earned the title of "Beijing 2022 Winter Olympics and Paralympics Transport Service Enterprise" granted by the Beijing 2022 Winter Olympics and Paralympics Traffic Command and Operation Control Center.

Beijing Beiqi Taxi Group Co., Ltd. was awarded the title of "Beijing Advanced Group for the Beijing 2022 Winter Olympics and Paralympics" by the CPC Beijing Municipal Committee and Beijing Municipal People's Government.

BPTC and the 12th Fleet of the Sixth Passenger Transport Branch obtained the title of "2022 Staff Library Demonstration Site" awarded by the All-China Federation of Trade Unions.

BPTC, the First Passenger Transport Branch, the Second Passenger Transport Branch, the Fourth Passenger Transport Branch, the Fifth Passenger Transport Branch, the Sixth Passenger Transport Branch, and the Seventh Passenger Transport Branch secured the title of "Municipal Transport Safety Advanced Unit" by the Beijing municipal traffic safety department joint conference in 2022.

Beijing Public Transport Tram Corporation was acclaimed as the 2020-2021 National "Ankang Cup" Competition Winner issued by the All-China Federation of Trade Unions and other agencies.

The case of "Inheriting the Legacy of BPTC, Keeping Our Original Aspirations-- Empowering Primary-level Party Building with the New 'Five Good' Practice" of the Party General Branch of the Zoo Hub Station Management Center of the Trolley Bus Branch was selected as one of the Top 10 Primary-level Party Building Innovation Cases in the Transportation Industry.

The Second Passenger Transport Branch received the "2022 Capital Labor Certificate" from the Beijing Federation of Trade Unions.

Route 877 of the 3rd Fleet of the Eighth Passenger Transport Branch gained the title of "Beijing Worker Pioneer" from the Beijing Federation of Trade Unions.

The Male High-Quality Service Demonstration Team of the Third Passenger Transport Branch was recognized as one of the top 10 "Safe Transport Service Providers • Beijing Role Models" collectives by the Beijing Municipal Commission of Transport.

Our employees' honors and accolades (partial)

Nian Zhikuan from the Sixth Passenger Transport Branch was awarded the 2022 National May Day Labor Medal of the All-China Federation of Trade Unions and the 2022 "Beijing Youth Role Model" of the Beijing Municipal Committee of the Communist Youth League of Beijing.

Cui Man from the Fifth Passenger Transport Branch attained the title of the 21st "National Youth Expert" awarded by the Central Committee of the Communist Youth League of China and the Ministry of Human Resources and Social Security.

Wang Chao, from the Publicity Department of BPTC, was nominated for the News Maker Award at the 9th "SOE Good News" event hosted by the News Center of the SASAC and the Central SOE Media Alliance.

Kou Jing, Xu Long, and Zhao Shiwen from the Publicity Department of BPTC, and Yang Sheng from the Trolley Bus Branch won the first prize of the 2021 Beijing professional news award by the Beijing Journalism Society.

Wang Zhi, Deputy Manager of the Safety Service Department of the Eighth Passenger Transport Branch, received the title of the Beijing 2022 Winter Olympics and Paralympics Transport Service Advanced Individual, the Beijing 2022 Winter Olympics and Paralympics Beijing Advanced Individual, the Beijing Municipal Work Safety Advanced Individual, and the Beijing Municipal Commission of Transport's Top 30 Individuals of Safe Transport Service Providers • Beijing Role Models.

Seven employees, including Du Jianping, driver of Route 695 of the First Passenger Transport Branch, won the "Capital Labor Medal" from the Beijing Federation of Trade Unions.

Sun Qifeng, driver of the 18th Fleet of the Third Passenger Transport Branch, acquired the title of "SOE • Beijing Model" in 2022 from the State-owned Assets Supervision and Administration Commission of People's Government of Beijing Municipality.

Chang Jingsheng, driver of the 11th Fleet of the Seventh Passenger Transport Branch, was acknowledged as a role model in the first week of August in the 2022 "Beijing Role Model" event hosted by the Publicity Department of the CPC Beijing Municipal Committee and the Capital Civilization Office.

Chen Meng and Liu Ran from the Third Passenger Transport Branch and Fan Lubin from the Fifth Passenger Transport Branch secured the title of "2022 Most Charming Voluntary Service Family in the Capital" from the Capital Civilization Committee.

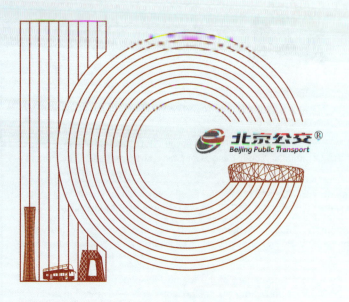

北京公交®
Beijing Public Transport

A Decade
Seeking Innovation and Aiming High

Running buses witness the passing of time and changes of a city. In the past decade, BPTC's buses have always been there for passengers from dawn to dusk. We have supported every major event in the capital and emerged with a new image through each transformation. Trials and tribulations have enabled BPTC to undergo transformative changes, through which we have grown stronger and forged ahead with our original aspirations. At a new starting point, BPTC will continue to serve all passengers and inject the strong vitality of BPTC into the development of the capital in the new era, making our running buses a pleasant sight that shines more brilliantly.

Contribution to UN SDGs

A Decade Highlighting Social Responsibility

For ten consecutive years, BPTC has disclosed CSR performance information. With dreams in mind, we hold up our heads, thoughtfully communicate the message of serving passengers, and write CSR stories meticulously. In the buses running toward a hopeful future, we join hands with more stakeholders.

A decade in numbers

With miles accumulating, passengers and buses converge. Numbers reflect our vigorous development, the rapid changes in the bus network in Beijing, and our commitment to serving people. They also indicate the significant economic, environmental, and social values that we create.

2013-2022

121.37 billion kilometers cumulative distance covered

1.214 billion kilometers travelled per year on average

Equivalent to **30,286** laps around the Earth a year

317.88 billion cumulative passenger trips served by buses and trolleybuses

3.179 billion passenger trips severed per year on average

Equivalent to transporting **3.97** times the world's population in ten years

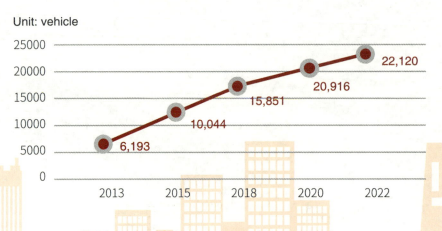

Unit: vehicle

6,193   10,044   15,851   20,916   22,120

2013   2015   2018   2020   2022

Total number of clean energy and new energy buses

e optimized the report fra-
ework, condensed the cha-
er on CSR performance,
creased the share of empl-
ee stories and CSR stories,
riching the concept of CSR.

2021

We invited more stakeholders to participate in the reporting preparation. We systematically displayed the changes and historical leapfrog over the years in the technical equipment, operations and services, transport services for major events, and talent training of the centenary BPTC. Based on more flexible and diverse design, it showed our commitment to working with more partners for a bright future.

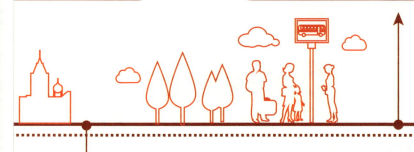

For the first time, we set two CSR features, connected the report contents in the structure of "past-present-future", depicted the bright prospects of the next 100 years, and released the report to the world for the first time in a Chinese and English live stream, improving our CSR system.

2022

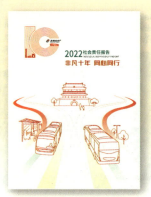

Ten years on, our original aspirations remain unchanged. The tenth report is a summary and also a new beginning, structurally highlighting the key actions of the last decade in innovative transformation. The 2022 report disclosed our rich CSR measures, illuminating our CSR journey forward.

Interwined networks
connecting passengers

◎In 2013,

we took the lead in launching a customized bus service model in China, which was well-received by passengers and all walks of life.

◎In 2019,

by improving public transport infrastructure in every village of Fangshan District and other places, we facilitated rural reform and innovation and made contribution to Beijing's urban-rural integrated development.

◎In 2020,

the ceremony of undertaking bus services in the Beijing Economic-Technological Development Area and launching the operation of the ETOWN subsidiary was held.

◎In 2014,

we restructured the night bus network.

◎In 2019,

BPTC held the signing ceremony of the handover of Xianglong Bus with Beijing Xianglong Assets Management Co., Ltd., realizing the integrated operation of bus services in the urban districts of Beijing.

◎In 2021,

on-demand shuttle buses were put into operation to meet the short-distance travel needs of passengers in six areas such as Wangjing and Universal Beijing Resort.

◎In 2015,

we signed a strategic cooperation agreement with the People's Government of Fangshan District to take over Beijing Kaijiefeng Public Traffic Passenger Transportation Co., Ltd.

◎In 2020,

we won the bid for the scheduled shuttle bus routes to the Xiong'an High-Speed Railway Station and implemented the first bus operation service project in the completed zone of the Xiong'an New Area.

◎In 2022,

we officially undertook all 70 bus routes in the Tongzhou District to further integrate Beijing's ground public transport.

Multi-story bus depots and modern hubs
offering comprehensive and stable service

◎In 2013,

Wuzhuang Bus Depot, the first standardized demonstration bus depot, was officially put into operation.

◎In 2018,

Wangzuo bus maintenance facility – Beijing's first such facility started construction.

◎In 2021,

the Shiyuan Bus Terminal supporting the Universal Beijing Resort was completed.

◎In 2016,

Beijing's first multi-story bus parking building started construction at the Maguanying Bus Depot.

◎In 2019,

Yanqing Comprehensive Transport Service Center (bus depot and maintenance center) started construction.

◎In 2022,

the construction of the main bus terminal in the west of the cultural and tourism zone in the Tongzhou District was completed.

◎In 2017,

the first mechanical parking building for pure electric buses in China, the Ertongchang bus parking building, started construction.

◎In 2020,

Beijing's first multi-story bus P+R (park and ride) parking facility – Guogongzhuang Bus Depot and multi-story parking building project was completed.

◎In 2022,

the Liuniangfu Bus Terminal started construction.

A Decade of Reform and Development for People

Our reform responds to people's needs. Bearing in mind the original aspiration of serving the people, we march forward to pursue innovation, dedicate ourselves to the cause of the Party and the state. We understand what passengers need, wholeheartedly contribute to urban transport, and seek development and breakthroughs with a broad vision in mind. Tracking the needs of the people for better transport services, we aim to transform BPTC into a tech-intensive modern integrated service provider of passenger transport.

New development momentum generated by digital transformation

Digital transformation is an all-encompassing, systematic, whole-process and strategic project that fosters new competitive edges for the future. In the past ten years, in response to the new digital transport trend, we have employed emerging technologies such as 5G, Internet of Things, artificial intelligence, blockchain, cloud computing, big data, edge computing, etc., to promote the in-depth integration and wide application of digital technology. In this process, we have adopted data-centered, networked, and platform-driven approaches, and started our efforts from new infrastructure, technologies, and scenarios. These efforts help update bus operation products and services and accelerate the modernization process of BPTC.

Digital transformation is crucial to promoting the high-quality development of BPTC and providing high-quality public transport services, which also improves the value of public transport.

We have gradually consolidated the foundation of digitalization, built a "digital cloud platform" and a "data lake", and formed an overall digital structure consisting of "one bus cloud platform, six business application platforms, and four supporting systems". At the same time, we have built and improved 75 IT-based management systems including thoses for operation control, dispatching, ticket management, vehicle resources, material management, human resources, financial management, and legal management. They inject digital vitality into the Corporation, improve work efficiency, and drive change with digitalization.

A decade of digital transformation reflects our lasting pursuit and response to the times. It also shows our unswerving mission and responsibility to meet the needs of passengers for better travel services.

Guided by the "bus + Internet" thinking, we fully adopt relevant technologies and have established a real-time and dynamic travel information forecasting system and developed a mobile application that provides services such as travel planning, arrival reminders, route inquiries, and bus crowdedness inquiries. The application has so far registered 26 million users. In terms of the shift in operation control, informed by passenger data, we have realized automatic planning, intelligent scheduling, and dynamic operation control by digitalizing operation and management. As a result, 702 scattered operation control units are condensed into 41 regional integrated intelligent operation control centers. The average number of trips coordinated through operation control has been increased to 476, with 99% of planned trips realized and a departure punctuality rate of more than 98%.

In the future, driven by digitalization, we will continue to explore new directions, models, and mechanisms for a digitalized public transport corporation. We will integrate digital means with different business processes and build new infrastructure to empower the transition of traditional one to realize the transformation toward digital public transport and lead the innovative and sustainable development of the public transport industry.

BPTC Operational Dispatch Control Center

Shaoyaoju Regional Intelligent Operation Control Center of the First
Passenger Transport Branch

Regional Intelligent Operation Control Center of the Nanwu
Region of the Trolley Bus Branch

Express direct route

Shared customized route

Customized bus route

On-demand shuttle bus

More flexible bus routes enable better services

Committed to delivering better public transport services to more people, BPTC leads the public transport mode and improves the quality of life in cities. We diversify public transport services by launching a variety of products, uphold our passenger-centered aspirations with the sincerest actions, and promote BPTC's century-old culture and legacy. By enriching passenger transport services, we expand urban transport space and offer flexible, differentiated, and high-quality travel solutions for passengers.

BPTC is the first in China to launch flexible and customized bus routes, reflecting the service concept of tailored and on-demand services.

In April 2011, together with Changping District Transport Bureau, we launched the community commute express bus service with reserved seats in the two major communities of Tiantongyuan and Huilongguan. It is our initial practice of flexible bus routes that offered insight into customized bus services.

In August 2013, before the successful launch of customized business bus routes, we organized a professional team of nearly 100 members to survey more than 100 residential areas and office buildings, from which we better understood the scale of communities, location, traffic conditions, bus stops, and the best routes to be planned. Be it Changping in the north, Daxing in the south, Fangshan in the west, or Yanjiao in the east, our survey personnel investigated all the locations where passengers were expected to gather. Meanwhile, our employees responsible for the development of a customized bus platform and relevant information services worked day and night before their launch to the public. On September 9, 2013, China's first customized business bus route was put into operation on the Jingtong Expressway, ushering in flexible bus services for BPTC. This was an innovative approach for BPTC to facilitate personalized travel, help alleviate traffic congestion, and lead green transport.

The continuous expansion of flexible bus routes helps improve the quality of public transport services, practice the concept of "Mobility as Life", and realize the shift from "crowding public transport", "taking public transport", to "enjoying public transport".

Later, flexible bus services such as the express direct route, holiday route, high-speed rail express route, leisure tourism route, shared customized route, dedicated route to Capital Institute of Pediatrics, and other demand-responsive bus routes were launched one after another. In addition, the customized bus route application, website, WeChat platform, mini-program, and other terminals were put into use, allowing passengers to efficiently book travel at any time and boosting the customization experience. While maximizing the benefits of intensive public transport, improving ground public transport, and meeting the multi-level travel needs of residents, we have enabled passengers to feel a greater sense of gain in urban development.

Mr. Gao, a frequent on-demand shuttle buses user, said: "I take the on-demand shuttle buses to the subway station, get on the train, and walk straight to my office after getting off. The on-demand shuttle buses is the major way for me to move from my community to the subway station. Since it is convenient and comfortable, I take it almost every day during the morning and evening rush hours."

People enjoy their travel in the foreseeable future.

Against the new trend of urban transport development, we will unleash the potential of supply, understand the needs of passengers, innovate in service models with more products, and see our flexible transport services better match people's needs. We will create diverse transport services that improve people's sense of gain and well-being, helping achieve high-quality development and high-quality services, and efficient governance of public transport in the capital.

Providing accessible public transport services

As a symbol of civilization, public transport accessibility concerns the people's sense of gain, happiness, and security, reflects the realization of a country with a strong transportation network, and is linked to the well-being of hundreds of millions of families. Dedicated to building a bridge connecting every member of society to the outside world, we aim to allow physically challenged people to go outside, engage in social activities, and show their self-worth. From the improvement of barrier-free facilities to the optimization of our services, we constantly tackle real-world issues in public transport accessibility.

In modern times, society and people both call for public transport accessibility. To meet the needs of urban development and people's travel, BPTC has improved barrier-free facilities and optimized accessible services continuously.

As society ages, there is a growing demand for accessible, inclusive, and safe travel. By the end of 2022, people aged 60 and above in Beijing had reached 4.651 million, thus making public transport a preferred way of travel for more elderly people. When it comes to improving public transport accessibility, it is our priority to put in place barrier-free travel services featuring wide coverage, high-degree safety, and smooth connectivity and create an inclusive public transport system for all groups.

The holding of the 2008 Summer Olympics and 2022 Winter Olympics in Beijing offers an opportunity for us to integrate accessible services on a large scale. Especially in 2019, Beijing launched a campaign on public transport accessibility, prompting us to improve barrier-free services, awareness, and ability. We met the task of offering barrier-free bus services during the Beijing 2022 Winter Olympics and Paralympics, gaining considerable experiences public transport accessibility.

We are meticulous and serious in every detail, making public transport accessibility no longer a slogan but a commitment of BPTC to groups with special needs.

The construction and improvement of facilities is the first step in public transport accessibility. We have increased investment in purchasing barrier-free vehicles and renovating bus stops and stations, optimized the design of existing routes, flexibly adjusted operation, improved the barrier-free service model of bus stops and carriages, and created high-quality barrier-free demonstration routes. In addition, we optimized facilities such as handrails, ground anchors, barrier-free pedals, etc., and developed barrier-free guidance systems to help elderly and disabled passengers. Now, we have put into use more than 14,000 low-floor vehicles,

Buses with ramps are convenient for seniors in wheelchairs

Helping the elderly get on a low-floor bus

Buses with ramps are convenient for disabled passengers in wheelchairs

Helping people with disabilities to fix their wheelchairs on the bus

Buses pull over 50-cm away from the bus stop, facilitating barrier-free travel

including more than 12,000 vehicles with ramps. The barrier-free buses in the urban area account for more than 80% of the fleet, with six routes recommended as Beijing barrier-free demonstration routes. At the same time, through better exchanges with the Beijing Municipal Commission of Transport, the Beijing Disabled Persons' Federation, and the Beijing Municipal Office for Aging, we repeatedly study how to optimize the design of accessible services and carry out education and special rectification activities on a regular basis. With the standard of wheels 50cm away from the bus stop, we improved drivers' skills of pulling over parallel to the bus stop and give them frequent training to let them understand the inconvenience of the elderly and other groups. With the help of operational big data, we identified the routes and times that have the most elderly passengers and established an accessibility file of important routes and bus stops to improve services in a more targeted manner.

Barrier-free travel requires both physical and emotional connections to the outside world. It is not just about whether we have barrier-free facilities. What should we focus on is whether barrier-free services are good or excellent enough.

Under the guidance of the CPC Beijing Municipal Committee and Beijing Municipal People's Government on creating a barrier-free environment of respecting the elderly and helping the disabled, we have built an accessible service management system with a new accessibility management model that the top leadership of BPTC take a leading role, the top leadership of our subsidiaries play a supervisory role, and fleet managers are responsible for implementation. Additionally, we organize activities to "respect the elderly and help the disabled" and strengthen publicity, fostering a strong service atmosphere of care for the elderly and the disabled in the BPTC system and society. By doing so, we improve the travel experience of elderly and disabled passengers and make barrier-free travel common and dignified.

We will bring warmth to every passenger with future-oriented inclusion and continuous progress.

It is the responsibility of all and the mission of BPTC as the capital's ground public transport operator to create an all-age-friendly and barrier-free travel environment that benefits everyone. In the future, we will build on our efforts to develop barrier-free facilities used during the 2008 Summer Olympics and 2022 Winter Olympics periods, uphold the excellent traditional Chinese culture, and employ advanced technology and equipment to create a barrier-free travel environment for elderly and disabled passengers. This will make the capital a city for barrier-free travel for all ages and lead the national efforts in promoting public transport accessibility.

The Government Service Center of the Beijing Municipal Commission of Transport inspected the "efficient handling of complaints" of BPTC

Work meeting about "efficient handling of complaints" held in May

Personnel serve in the bus stop

"Efficient handling of complaints" management center

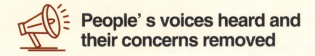

People's voices heard and their concerns removed

Case — Listening attentively and exploring with feet, just for the convenience of passengers' travel

"I live in the Xinbei community. I used to walk a long way to take Route 508. Now it is almost on my doorstep, which is convenient. I would like to give a thumbs-up to the efficiency of BPTC!" Mr. Liu, a senior citizen, said. This is the recognition to BPTC for adding a bus stop after resident report the situation of going a long way to get the bus via the hotline of efficient handling of complaints. This means a lot to our staff handling passenger complaints. It is always our passion and the source of motivation to answer people's expectations.

Amid the innovative and profound reform of urban governance in the new era, a hotline brings together people's voices. As a public service enterprise operating Beijing's ground public transport and facilitating people's travel, BPTC set up an "efficient handling of complaints" management center in 2019 to better serve passengers, meet their demands, and increase their satisfaction.

Passenger travel matters to every family and carries the dreams of people and the memories of cities. That is why we attach importance to every complaint of passengers and pay close attention to every key detail.

Guided by passengers' demands, we serve passengers with concrete actions, solve their problems through effective channels, and strive to build trust and a bridge of communication between BPTC and passengers. We implement a 24/7 mechanism that allows rapid responses of "immediate verification on the same day, reply in three days, and conclusion and reporting in five days". To verify a complaint, we make collaborative consultation among multiple departments so that we can offer timely feedback to passengers and ensure that every issue will be responded timely.

When dealing with the complaint of passengers, action is the greatest sincerity.

We will carefully check and qualify each complaint, and keep in close contact with various departments. We integrate the data analysis of "efficient handling of complaints" into route adjustment and bus scheduling and use it to conduct bus route evaluation, the optimization of decision-making support, and route optimization follow-up, making route optimization more credible. Centering around the routes and time periods that receive most passenger complaints, we clarify the work responsibilities of personnel at all levels and the business process of opening, adjusting, or canceling routes in detail to improve our service quality.

In 2022, with the improvement of infrastructure and the influx of a large population, the demand for transfer continues to increase in the Yangtuo and Sanjiadian areas near the West Sixth Ring Road. After receiving requests from citizens, we conducted multiple on-site surveys, visited passengers at key bus stops, and solicited opinions from residents in nearby communities to carefully understand their actual needs for the specific direction of the line, stop settings, departure time, etc. We designed a route from Yangtuo to the east of Jin'an Bridge. A new line connecting Mentougou District and Shijingshan District. After more than two months of joint efforts, we have completed the bus schedules, posting of vehicle signs, and setting of stop posts and signs. The official opening of Route 502 has enabled rapid travel between areas such as Yangtuo, Junzhuang, and Sanjiadian in Mentougou District and Shijingshan District, shortening commuting time and facilitating public transportation for passengers.

We have shifted to the approach of "active governance, actions before complaints, and one-stop measures" to get to the bottom of public opinions based on in-depth analysis.

On a daily, weekly, monthly, and quarterly basis, we gather passengers' opinions to improve services in a targeted manner. For example, we get to know what are the top ten problems reflected by passengers, how they evolve, and how they are handled by relevant departments. It is hoped that the resolution of one problem can offer solutions to similar problems. In addition, we regularly analyze the types and trends of passengers' opinions with targeted responses. We study complaint cases and the risks of potential complaints, hoping to improve passengers' happiness, sense of gain, and sense of security by prediction and precautions. In 2022, 99.14% of complaints were resolved, an increase of 4.83% year on year, and the satisfaction rate was 99.11%, a year-on-year increase of 3.41%, gradually achieving better and faster responses.

"Efficient handling of complaints" is ongoing, and we will not stop the efforts.

The year 2023 is the fourth year in the reform of "efficient handling of complaints". For the four years, our service hotline has connected passengers across the city, shortening the distance between BPTC and passengers, which enables us to get passengers' understanding, support, and trust. In the future, we will always listen and respond to the voices of passengers, extract useful experience to support practice, and encourage passengers to engage in the governance of ground public transport to ensure joint contribution, governance, and sharing with more stakeholders.

Message from the expert:
At a fresh starting point, creating a new future

Wang Xianjin, Member of the National Committee of the Chinese People's Political Consultative Conference, Vice President and Chief Engineer of the China Academy of Transportation Sciences

Public transport, the critical infrastructure of a city, matters to people's well-being and serves as an important symbol of urban civilization and progress.

A century on, the public transport services provided by BPTC have achieved wide geographical coverage, inclusion, and urban-rural integration, making great contributions to the high-quality development of public transport in the capital. China Academy of Transportation Sciences cooperated with BPTC several times. We participate in, witness, and benefit from the development of BPTC. In recent years, with the rapid development of urban public transport, more diverse passenger demand and greener and smarter vehicles have raised higher requirements for bus operators.

- -

To alleviate traffic congestion, travel inconvenience, and environmental pollution, China has paid increasing attention to the strategy of "prioritizing urban public transport". In recent years, documents such as the *Outline for Building China's Strength in Transport* and *the National Comprehensive Three-dimensional Transportation Network Planning Outline* have pointed out the direction for implementing the strategy of "prioritizing urban public transport" in depth.

Against such a policy environment, it is necessary to deeply understand the expectations and demands of different stakeholders when it comes to prioritizing public transport. For the government, prioritizing public transport is to put public transport development high on the agenda of urban construction by allocating necessary resources to the development of public transport, including land resources such as roads, bus depots and etc. For the public, prioritizing public transport means right-of-way for buses, including frequently used school buses and shuttle buses. At the same time, it also means that the price of public transport is reasonable and affordable. Only by ensuring supply meets demand in a targeted manner can BPTC engage all parties to serve the strategy of prioritizing public transport.

Wang Xianjin led a team to BPTC for cross-party joint research activities

As digitalization and intelligence sweep across all industries, digital transformation has become a strategic imperative for the public transport industry to switch to new growth drivers and upgrade itself.

In recent years, BPTC has been employing the intelligent operation control system to improve bus speed and making use of big data technology to analyze the passenger flow of bus routes. This helps meet the needs of the public for transport services and improve the efficiency of resource allocation by the government, which is the goal pursued in digital transformation. Generally speaking, there is still some room to improve in BPTC's digital transformation, mainly in the following five aspects. First, it is necessary to consolidate the digital foundation and shore up infrastructure and basic resources. Second, BPTC should leverage the leading role of data applications to build data centers. Third, it is necessary to understand the requirements of data flow, break data silos, and truly realize data sharing. Fourth, a traffic data market should be fostered. Fifth, it is important to strengthen data security. These measures can help establish a systematic understanding of digital transformation and bring digital development to a new level.

Talent is essential for the development of an industry. The Ministry of Transport attaches great importance to the talent development strategy and the policy of intellectual resource development of the entire transportation industry.

The general goal should be to accelerate efforts in building a sufficient, well-structured, reasonably distributed, and excellent talent team and the priority should be placed on urgently needed talent in urban public transport, intelligent transport, and comprehensive transport. In 2020, BPTC set up China's first postdoctoral research center in the public transport industry, a pioneering step that was crucial to the development of the industry. Based on diverse application scenarios, BPTC offers a favorable research environment for talent growth. It is hoped that BPTC will deepen the all-around development of talent, prioritize the introduction, training, and use of talent on all fronts, and retain talent with the incentives of a promising career, a sense of belonging, and reasonable incomes. Also, it is imperative to accelerate the translation of innovation achievements into productivity growth and enable postdoctoral researchers to play a greater role in empowering the transformation and high-quality development of the conventional public transport industry.

2022 marks the tenth year since BPTC released the first social responsibility report, which is a new starting point. It is our expectation that BPTC can continue to pursue innovation in the face of new challenges and build a new public transport network that is more passenger-oriented, healthier, safer, greener, and more sustainable.

Services
Taking Actions to Meet People's Needs

It is the century-old tradition of BPTC and the dedication of BPTC's employees to serve passengers meticulously. Committed to serving the people, we seek innovation-driven development while perfecting our service details. Day in and day out, we expand the space of travel and search for more possibilities for urban development, empowering every dream, big or small. This vividly shows that BPTC has no limit in offering services for people's limited-distance travel.

Urban Travel Facilitated by a Dense Network

Under the new requirements of "improving quality, reducing costs, and increasing efficiency" in the passenger transport service market, we have further improved the three-tier "corridor routes, general routes, and micro routes" network, carried out punctuality projects, and implemented key projects, such as the Huitian areas (Tiantongyuan and Huilongguan in Beijing) and Beijing Municipal Administrative Center and metro connection bus services. To optimize bus routes, we flexibly adjust the location of bus stops and operation time, ensure that public transport is integrated into the functions of the capital, and improve the coverage and punctuality rates of buses, all of which satisfy passengers.

539
Bus routes covered by punctuality program

98.83%
Bus departure punctuality rate

Optimization of the bus network

- In 2022, we opened, adjusted, or canceled 100 bus routes. Specifically, we opened 12 new routes, adjusted 78 routes, and canceled 10 routes.
- We increased the length of bus network by 82.5 kilometers, making travel convenient for residents of 118 communities.
- We reduced the length of redundant bus routes by 276 kilometers and reduced the number of redundant bus stops by 700.

Ensuring metro connection bus services

- We set up the Yushuzhuang bus stop of Metro Line 16 and a new stop for Route 678 on the temporary set-aside road to ensure access to the nearest metro station.
- In response to the opening of a new metro line, we studied and proposed the addition of bus stops for the Xueyuanqiao Station of the South Extension of the Changping Line.
- We adjusted the Route 49 and 845 metro connection services to deal with the construction of the temporary bus stop of Dongguantounan Station.
- We inspected the 1,023 entrances and exits of 361 metro stations in Beijing. Guided by the principle of "one policy for one station", we raised the proportion of bus stops 30 meters away from metro station exits.

Promoting the punctuality project

- We improved operational efficiency by introducing routes with fixed-point departure and strengthening schedule management.
- We piloted the halfway section punctuality program. In 210 bus routes, we allowed operators to use the intelligent operation control system to monitor vehicle punctuality.

2020—2022 Operational Indicator Table

	Index(unit)	2020	2021	2022
Routes in operation	Total number of routes in operation	1,214	1,225	1,299
	Number of conventional bus routes	1,207	1,217	1,291
	Length of conventional bus routes (km)	28,418.4	28,579.7	30,173.9
	Length of route network (km)	7,628.6	7,771.3	8,180.6
	Number of stations	18,834	19,262	20,469
Optimized route network	Total number of optimized routes	212	151	100
	Length of overlapping routes reduced (km)	470.7	384.6	276.0
	Number of overlapping stops cut	1,083	941	700
	Length of bus routes on the road not covered before (km)	167.8	142.7	82.5
	Number of communities benefited	440	186	118

More Travel Choices

Based on the different travel needs of passengers, we bring out a new development model with customized bus routes as the mainstay and other special bus services routes such as regional shuttle buses, to-school buses, sightseeing buses, medical-purpose buses, mountain shuttle buses, and customized express buses. While providing flexible, differentiated, and quality public transport services, we make each customized bus route a pleasant sight of Beijing. By the end of 2022, our customized bus routes had been available in 16 places, including Wangjing, Universal Beijing Resort, Sujiatuo, Jiugong, Fengtai Science and Technology Park, Huilongguan Area, Yongfeng, Zhuxinzhuang, ETOWN, Tiantongyuan, Xierqi, Shahe, Daoxiang Lake, Nanluogu Alley, Beishenshu, and Lize Financial Business District.

On-demand shuttle bus to the Lize Financial Business District

418
Customized bus routes

158
Flexible bus routes

Buses are crucial to urban travel, and in the future, we should accelerate the formation of full-coverage bus right-of-way for whole-process travel services, ensure the speed and reliability of public transport to make it more attractive and competitive, and explore large-scale, bookable public transport."

——Guo Jifu, President of Beijing Transport Institute

Integrated Development Empowered by Public Transport

Transport integration is the foundation of and first step to the coordinated development of the Beijing-Tianjin-Hebei region. Following the policy on the coordinated development of the Beijing-Tianjin-Hebei region, we integrate into the development of the Beijing-Tianjin-Hebei urban cluster and make several explorations in public transport. We continue to expand the public transport business. Guided by the principle of "channeling urban resources to develop suburban routes", we undertook regional bus routes in Tongzhou, another milestone in the integration of Beijing's bus routes across urban and suburban areas. We fully supported the planning and construction of public transport in the Xiong'an New Area and expanded the Rongcheng project scale to improve public transport services in Xiong'an, making Xiong'an New Area a smart transport demonstration zone integrating green waters, region-specific tourism, and ecological industries. All the efforts of BPTC will help make the integrated development of the Beijing-Tianjin-Hebei region a reality.

19
Route concessions obtained in the Xiong'an New Area

3
Customized bus routes opened in the Xiong'an New Area

347.1 km
Total length of bus routes in the Xiong'an New Area

146
Vehicles operated in the Xiong'an New Area

Xiong'an Rongcheng Route 303 was put into operation

Spotlight

BPTC undertakes and transforms bus routes in Tongzhou District

We continue to promote the in-depth integration of the "two networks" so that the transfer between metro and buses is smoother and more comfortable, achieving greater public transport connectivity. We strive to build a service community through joint contributions and give full play to the pioneering role of BPTC in promoting the integrated development of the Beijing-Tianjin-Hebei region.

— Lin Qing, Deputy Director of Beijing Tongzhou District Bureau of Transport

In 2022, BPTC took charge of all bus routes in the Tongzhou District, providing a solid foundation and strong support for building a fast, convenient, efficient, and interconnected transport network at a faster pace and promoting the integrated development of the Beijing-Tianjin-Hebei region.

Since February 2021 when the Tongzhou District People's Government and BPTC set up a task force, the two sides have analyzed the operation of buses, bus stop layout, business operation and future direction of Tongzhou public transport after reform. We also established a weekly meeting mechanism, which lasted one and a half years, had more than 100 meetings that made breakthroughs around key issues such as the arrangement of employees, vehicles, bus stops, and bus routes, one by one.

On June 1, 2022, BPTC officially undertook all 70 bus routes covering an area of 906 square kilometers in the Tongzhou District. Tongzhou buses had brand-new vehicle models, energy mix, bus stop poles and signs, and bus shelters, helping realize the integration of Beijing's ground public transport. These efforts also laid a solid foundation for the formation of a new pattern of capital public transport development

featuring "one map", "one network", "one standard", and "one set of systems".

When the bus network in the Beijing Municipal Administrative Center changed overnight on June 1, passengers could not adapt to the new operation model. Attaching great importance to the issue, BPTC's leadership at all levels took a survey about passengers' needs at important bus stops and took swift actions to resolve passengers' travel requests and queries so that they could have a good travel experience.

The purpose of Beijing-Tianjin-Hebei transport integration is to benefit the majority of people by facilitating their travel, work, and life. Since BPTC undertook the bus lines of the Tongzhou District, the efforts made by BPTC have enhanced the functions of the area, coordinated urban-rural development, and played a vital role in promoting transport integration. Buses in the Tongzhou district have also become more convenient, attractive, and safer.

Since BPTC undertook the bus operation in the Tongzhou District, BPTC has improved the efficiency of operations, brought in new energy buses, and employed technology to ensure driving safety and management, making the bus network of the entire Tongzhou District more reasonable and bus operation smoother. In addition, we have integrated Tongzhou's time-honored culture with the corporate culture of the century-old BPTC by designing bus interiors with Tongzhou characteristics on multiple routes and creating a unique bus culture belonging to the Beijing Municipal Administrative Center. This has brought a completely upgraded public transport experience to Tongzhou residents.

Improving the operation and service

According to the "one policy for one route" principle, we have improved the operation and service of 45 routes, adjusted the operation time and intervals between buses to varying degrees, thus improving the bus network.

Greener bus fleet

We brought in 565 new energy buses, optimized the energy mix of vehicles so that 100% of buses in the Tongzhou District after integration are new energy vehicles, and leveled up vehicle comfort, eco-friendliness, and safety.

Upgrading facilities effectively

We have formulated plans for the standardized renovation of bus depots and the renewal of bus shelters, accelerated the upgrading of bus stop facilities, and made full use of electronic stop signs and smartphone applications to provide passengers with real-time and accurate departure time, arrival time, bus crowdedness, vehicle location, and other information.

Realizing regional intelligent operation control

We have established the regional intelligent operation control center of the Beijing Municipal Administrative Center, put more efforts into digitalizing operation control of public transport in the Tongzhou District, and relied on the newly built Shiyuan Bus Terminal, a regional intelligent operation control center, to realize regional intelligent operation control.

Officially undertaking bus operation of the Tongzhou District

New energy vehicles in the Tongzhou District

Bus interior with Tongzhou characteristics

The operation control center located at Shiyuan Bus Terminal, Tongzhou District

Digital Transformation for Smart Mobility

With an emphasis on the in-depth integration of digital technology into operation management, we continue to concentrate our efforts on smart and digital public transport, and apply the achievements of digitalization widely, to transform the operation control model. Also, we put in place electronic bus stop signs and diversify transport scenarios to allow pleasant and unhindered travel in a digitalized setting.

We have released the Smart Bus 2.0 and 3.0 versions of digital application capability packages.

With the support of the data lake, we promote machine iteration to advance intelligent upgrading and digitalize the operation control system, gradually shaping a regional operation control system with "simplified hierarchy, clear rights and responsibilities, intelligence and efficiency".

We have efficiently upgraded the bus card reader and built a health status verification platform.

We have developed a pole QR code information generation and query system.

We have built the application scenario of digital RMB and allowed the connection of multiple payment channels.

The intelligent ignition system and vehicle CAN data application monitoring and analysis system are in operation.

1,815

Electronic bus stop signs put in place

Case Intelligent operation control ensured travel on the first day of school

On September 1, 2022, Beijing's primary and secondary schools welcomed a new school year. This also meant a significant increase in the number of parents and students during the morning and evening rush hours. Therefore, the 41 regional intelligent operation control centers of BPTC, based on the information system, strengthened remote operation control and conducted real-time monitoring of road congestion, vehicle crowdedness, driving distance, etc. More than 600 spare vehicles at over 240 bus depots were arranged, which put into operation given road congestion and bus route operation, with an aim to reduce waiting time and ensure sufficient capacity and traffic order.

The digital management interface of BPTC's operation service

Safety at Every Stop

Travel safety is one of the constituents of a happy urban life. Committed to the philosophy of "People First, Life Foremost", BPTC works to safeguard transport security against bad weathers throughout the year. Focusing on details, the Company makes every effort to fulfill safety responsibilities and defuse potential safety risks, only to ensure smooth bus operation and safe travel.

Mile by mile: A commitment to safety

Remaining true to its original aspiration, BPTC works cautiously to ensure safe travels. We integrate driving safety into our daily routines by minimizing any potential risk to smooth travels so as to provide safe and reliable travel experience for every passenger.

In 2022, BPTC issued the Work Plan of Building a Modern Driving Safety Management System to build a management system for driving safety at a faster pace, enhance risk control capacity and the application of the smart security system and modernize our driving safety management comprehensively.

Approximately

8,000

Vehicles installed with Advanced Driver Assistance System accumulatively

5,750

Vehicles equipped with abnormal behavior recognition system accumulatively

2,150

Multi-sign emotion sensing devices offered for drivers on key high-speed lines, night shift lines and the Beijing Municipal Administrative Center line accumulatively

We pay attention to drivers' physical conditions and encourage drivers to take their physical examinations as required in time. We complete driver's psychological archives and organize general tests of their psychological adaptability.

We developed a biorhythm management system for drivers to set up a driver safety warning model and a mental stress perception model.

Measures to ensure driving safety

We have launched a real-time voice call system for drivers on the night shift and provide multi-sign emotion sensing devices for drivers on key high-speed lines, night shift lines and the Beijing Municipal Administrative Center line.

We trialed and popularized the A-pillar blind spot warning system to reduce the adverse impact of blind spots with the help of technology.

The one-button alert system self-examined 21,500 times, covering all major traffic lines.

Night driving safety inspection

Pre-job oath-taking

Friendly reminder on summer fatigue

Friendly reminder on the driving safety on snowy day

 Case ## BPTC equiped drivers with emotion sensing bands

In June, 2022, BPTC officially undertook the bus operation of the Tongzhou District. To ensure the safety of passengers and drivers, BPTC dispensed emotion sensing bands to all drivers in Tongzhou, which can pre-warn drivers' abnormal physical and mental conditions. Emotion sensing bands can not only monitor drivers' vital signs including body temperature, heart rate, respiratory rate, blood oxygen level, exercise frequency, blood pressure and sleep quality in real time, but also their emotions such as depression and anxiety, safeguarding their mental health around the clock. Should any anomalies occur in drivers' physical values before or during departure, the fleet manager will send relevant personnel to get their health status and ask them to seek medical treatment and take a rest. If necessary, shifts or sick leave would be allowed for indisposed drivers to ensure safe travel environment for Tongzhou residents.

A driver wearing a multi-sign emotion sensing device

More guarantee, more reassuring

Accidents arise out of negligence of details. We foster red line awareness and stick to it to improve our safety management system, enhance emergency response capacity and strengthen identification of hidden risks. We work to improve staff safety management quality across the board, make every effort to build a high wall against safety risks to public transport and to the well-being of thousands of households.

○ Cementing safety foundation

- BPTC is committed to improving its institutional structure, security capacity, technology strength and multilateral cooperation in targeted areas, to build a modern driving safety management system.
- We revised some safety management rules such as the *Regulations on Public Security and Fire Prevention Management at Bus Parking Stations.*
- In July 2022, BPTC passed the Level-One Work Safety Standardization.

○ Identifying and defusing hidden risks

- We have established the work safety inspection system to standardize the inspection procedure.
- We enhanced the application of information system to work safety inspection, such as, applying the risk identification information system to troubleshoot work safety risks.
- We continued the investigation into safety risks to natural gas use and housing safety and advance the special rectification to eliminate all kinds of hidden dangers in time.
- We continued our three-year action plan on work safety.

○ Improving emergency response

- We have effectively publicized and implemented newly revised contingency plans, strengthened staff safety emergency training and rolled out emergency drills to improve our warning and response capacity.
- We made coordinated plans to arrange emergency duty and response to special weathers such as flood and heavy snow.
- We standardized the inspection by staff on emergency duty and improve the overall management of work safety.

3,413
Emergency cases on the bus handled, with

3,776
People involved

6,095
Emergency drills carried out, with

84,899
Participants

438
Emergency plans for secondary subsidiaries revised

2020—2022 Support of Personnel, Facilities and Technology

	Project	2020	2021	2022
Personnel	Number of bus safety management personnel	39,069	36,679	31,630
Facilities	Number of closed electronic fence	500	500	500
	Vehicles with one-button alert system	17,530	17,271	21,500
Technology	Vehicles with automatic identification system	15,600	17,249	24,043

Safety culture rooted in minds

BPTC puts the lives and safety of passengers in the first place. We organize a variety of special activities on safety culture and offer training and publicity events on safe travel, aiming to make it a code of conduct for employees and instill the safety culture into our staff's mind.

Safety education and training

We continue to promote safety education and training. We organize professional training sessions for drivers, conductors and safety management personnel. Regular training on safety are also held. We have unveiled the Collection of Warning Cases of Urban Public Transport Operation and carried out such events as the driving safety courseware competition, "Gold and Silver Steering Wheel Award" ceremony, oath-taking, safety-learning and note reviews, enriching the forms of safety education and communicating the idea of "Safe Beijing, Safe Transport" to all staff members.

Safety-themed activities

We organize various themed activities such as waiting at the zebra crossing, National Traffic Safety Day, work safety month, in an attempt to foster a strong atmosphere of safety culture and raise the awareness of employees and the public.

Release Ceremony of the *Collection of Warning Cases of Urban Public Transport Operation*

2022 "Gold and Silver Steering Wheel Award" Ceremony

248,000

Participants in safety education and training activities

200

Drivers won the Gold Steering Wheel Award, the highest honor for safe driving

1,232

Drivers won the Silver Steering Wheel Award

305

Publicity stations set up and

43,768

Knowledge manuals distributed on work safety publicity and consultation day and fire drills

The *Collection of Warning Cases of Urban Public Transport Operation* won the first prize in video category of the 2022 National Highway Excellent Popular Science Work by China Highway & Transportation Society.

Safety publicity and consultation day

 Case **BPTC celebrated National Traffic Safety Day**

On December 2, 2022, BPTC greeted the 11th National Traffic Safety Day with the theme of "Going home safe with responsible travel", on which education events were held to communicate the transport safety idea across the board. On that day, all passenger transport branches cooperated with traffic control departments in different jurisdictions to urge on-job drivers to strictly abide by traffic rules and regulations, such as giving precedence to pedestrians and being courteous and defensive in driving, through daily reminders, a letter to drivers and questionnaires on driving safety. In the meantime, the public was advocated to practice safe travel and maintain a safe, harmonious and orderly traffic environment and safe driving atmosphere.

Publicity activities on National Traffic Safety Day

A safe network

As new information technologies, including cloud computing, big data and Internet of Things, grow faster, the scale of public transport network is also expanding. Specifically, its independence and controllability are always the prerequisite for network security. We strengthen network security mechanisms to underpin network security and employ technical approaches to comprehensively monitor network security loopholes. Meanwhile, we continue to raise network security awareness and work to improve public transport network security awareness as well as defense and governance capacity, keeping a stable and controllable situation of network security.

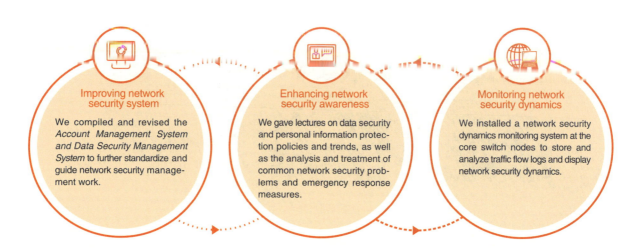

Improving network security system

We compiled and revised the *Account Management System and Data Security Management System* to further standardize and guide network security management work.

Enhancing network security awareness

We gave lectures on data security and personal information protection policies and trends, as well as the analysis and treatment of common network security problems and emergency response measures.

Monitoring network security dynamics

We installed a network security dynamics monitoring system at the core switch nodes to store and analyze traffic flow logs and display network security dynamics.

Network security measures

 Case | **BPTC trained employees to use licensed software**

In November 2022, BPTC carried out licensed software training for all employees, teaching them how to identify pirated software, explain the harm of piracy, its advantages and disadvantages and standardize the use of software, thus strengthening the awareness of intellectual property protection and information security. By now, all software on BPTC's systems and platforms has been licensed to ensure the stable operation of the Corporation's business systems, intelligent bus operation control platform, on-board ticket devices and information service facilities, and guarantee information security.

Licensed software training

Enjoyable Travel for Everyone

Bus routes may start or end somewhere but our warm services always continue. As a service-oriented enterprise, we take multiple measures to implement "efficient handling of complaints", and innovate in service methods to create a comfortable environment for passengers with cozy buses and considerate services. We provide high-quality services so that people can enjoy public transport.

Deepening "efficient handling of complaints"

Only by knowing what people think can we solve what matters most to them. Listening carefully to people's voices and complaints, we deepen the reform and innovation of "efficient handling of complaints" and strengthen the mechanism. In addition to regular reporting, regular notification, and early warnings, we optimize assessments and incentives and standardize and institutionalize "efficient handling of complaints" management. We also raise the awareness and ability of all subsidiaries to handle complaints and continue to carry out monthly activities of "efficient handling of complaints" with comprehensive management efforts to gradually move towards "proactive handling of potential complaints".

93.52%
Passenger satisfaction rate

13,377
Cases addressed through "efficient handling of complaints" decreased compared with 2021

21.95%
Percentage of case decrease

199,577 times
Customer communication (hotline, mailbox, visit, etc.)

661
Visits made to solve key, difficult, and most concerned issues

99.24 points
The overall evaluation of "efficient handling of complaints" averaged

An operator answers passengers' questions

Understanding needs via unhindered channels

To better serve passengers, we utilize multiple communication channels to listen to passengers' voices, understand their needs, and ensure immediate responses. We respond sincerely, speedily, professionally, and warmly to every passenger.

We visit bus stops, communities, and buses every month to talk with passengers and understand what they think.

We improve the handling of hotlines such as 12345 and 96166 to keep ourselves updated on passengers' needs and opinions.

We expand the use of new social media platforms by tapping into the potential of our website, WeChat, Weibo, Douyin, and other platforms to strengthen two-way interaction with passengers.

We organize "fans meetings", "public transport experts", and other activities to enhance communication with passengers and keep close contact with them.

Satisfying passengers with premium services

We upgrade our services, deeply explore the establishment of premium bus routes, and carefully design the 2.0 version of bus culture, so that buses can be the carrier of urban culture. Meanwhile, we regularly clean vehicles and offer special group services to meet passengers' needs for flexible, high-quality, and interactive travel services.

Case A special improvement project has upgraded service quality

To develop modern and passenger-oriented public transport that meets people's expectations for better travel, BPTC promoted a special improvement project. By implementing the key tasks of the eight improvement projects such as the service quality improvement project, we have made breakthroughs in service quality, operation, and development. With several service management measures in place, we raised employees' service awareness through special research, governance, competitions, and other activities. We also build demand-responsive bus routes, high-ridership bus routes, and barrier-free service demonstration bus routes to improve the quality of service to passengers.

Case The "Canal Culture Bus" of Route T116 offers a new travel experience

The Fifth Passenger Transport Branch and the Publicity Department of the Tongzhou District Party Committee have launched three "Canal Cultural Buses" on Route T116, providing a new option for tourists to go on holiday outings. Inspired by the cultural concept of the Beijing-Hangzhou Grand Canal, the "Canal Culture Bus" focuses on the tourist attractions of the Beijing Municipal Administrative Center, the history and culture of the Grand Canal, the concept of green development in various ways such as graphic display, cloud audio-visual presentations, sightseeing via code-scanning, dynamic lighting, etc. These measures offer tourists an enjoyable travel experience.

"It's great to take a bus around the Lvxin Forest Park and the bank of the Grand Canal, enjoying the beautiful scenery and the time-honored appeal of the 'Eight Scenic Spots of Tongzhou'."

—— Mr. Li, a passenger who lives in Tongzhou District

56,000+
Personnel organized for

136,000
Vehicle cleaning, with

12,000+
Signs replaced

52,000+
Safe trips of elderly and disabled passengers helped by BPTC

54
Bus routes designed with cultural interiors, covering

2,080
Vehicles

28
Premium service demonstration bus routes selected

300
Premium service demonstration buses selected

To promote the establishment of premium bus routes, we have formulated the BPTC Premium Bus Route Development Plan, to build a new system of diversified bus culture. We add QR code scanning services, and provide three-dimensional visual presentations to improve travel experiences.

Keeping in mind the actual needs of special groups such as the elderly, we maintain daily services and emergency plans and take multiple measures to improve barrier-free services to be more considerate.

We heighten service awareness, strengthen the management of "zero tolerance", "taboo prohibition", and the manager's response to passengers' complaints. Totally, we granted six quality service awards to employees.

We make vehicle cleaning more specialized and organize all subsidiaries to clean vehicles on the 20th of each month to create a clean and tidy environment for passengers.

Case

A new Route 1 offers the first "bus + cloud tourism" travel mode

On October 13, 2022, China Mobile Beijing and BPTC jointly launched a service innovation brand empowerment activity with the smart bus mini program "Cloud Travelling Route 1", creating a new "bus + tourism" culture that offers diverse travel experiences for the general public. The mini program includes three sections: a map, Route 1 introduction, and VR cloud tourism. With the hand-drawn map, passengers can listen to real-time introductions about important buildings and tourist spots along Route 1 and get to know the history of "China Red" via the QR code, bringing passengers a new Route 1 experience combining virtual reality and in-person engagement.

The mini program "Cloud Travelling Route 1"

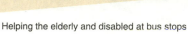

Helping the elderly and disabled at bus stops

A bus culture of respecting the elderly

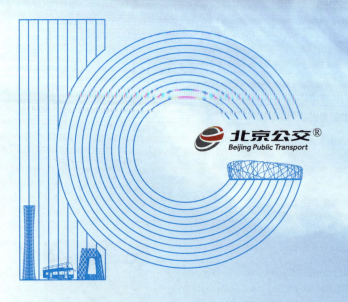

Responsibility

Dedicating Ourselves to Bus Operations

As the main player in Beijing's ground public transport, BPTC stays loyal to the Party and the state, helps address social concerns, and shoulders significant responsibilities in serving national political events and major ceremonies. With warm, sincere, quality, and thoughtful transport services, BPTC's employees improve the reputation of the Corporation on critical occasions, showing to the capital residents and the world the image of a public transport corporation of a major country.

Contribution to UN SDGs

Transport Services for Beijing 2022 Winter Olympics

Beijing 2022 Winter Olympics kicked off with "snowflake" on the Start of Spring, a solar term in China that marks the end of winter and the beginning of the spring. Seizing the development opportunities presented by the great era, we adopted the highest standards to guarantee transport facilities, intelligent and efficient operation control, accurate and powerful safety plans, and considerate travel services helped us complete the task of offering transport services to the Beijing 2022 Winter Olympics and Paralympics. Our actions demonstrated the responsibility of BPTC's employees and provided a new benchmark for transport services for major events.

BPTC was awarded the "Outstanding Contribution Collective for Beijing 2022 Winter Olympics and Paralympics" by the CPC Central Committee and the State Council.

Stronger leadership and thoughtful arrangements and implementation

We established a Beijing 2022 command center headed by major leaders of the Corporation and other key members as the deputy commanders, and sent excellent managers, operation control personnel, drivers, and maintenance workers to serve Beijing 2022.

Excellent operation services and measures in place

We maintained an operation control mechanism and strengthened operation monitoring. We optimized bus schedules and ensured departure and arrival punctuality rates of more than 99%. We enhanced emergency preparedness with 39 emergency support tasks completed.

Technology empowerment and multiple measures taken

Supported by digital technology, we realized the immediate uploading of real-time collected data such as vehicle position, speed, and image and built a Beijing 2022 bus operation control system.

Solid bottom-line awareness and sense of responsibility

We assessed the risk of transport services comprehensively and formulated emergency plans. We organized personnel of different groups in drills to improve their capabilities. We also strengthened process control to ensure no mistakes.

Drivers offering transport services to the Yanqing competition zone of the Beijing 2022 solemnly took an oath

Transport services to the Beijing 2022

Vehicle drills for special weather emergencies

Rescue vehicles for Beijing 2022

Case   Extraordinary actions ensure safety

As an SOE in the capital, BPTC resolutely assumed the responsibility of offering transport services for the Beijing 2022 Winter Olympics and Paralympics and organized personnel to the Xiaohaituo Mountain 12 times to inspect the route. We also drew a safe route map of Xiaohaituo and compiled the Regulations on Road Safety in the Xiaohaituo Mountain Area. A special weather suspension mechanism and a closed-loop system for handling accidents were established. During Bejing 2022, the Yanqing team kept checking the traffic conditions of the Xiaohaituo Mountain at 4 a.m. every day. This routine helped them identify potential safety hazards and come up with safe driving measures for special weather and special road sections to ensure overall safety and stability in ground public transport, helping BPTC accomplish the task of offering transport services.

Drivers in the Yanqing competition zone received training on safe driving on mountain roads

Listen the Snowflake is Cheering (excerpt)
—— Lei Chao and Fang Yuanyuan

In 2022, "A snowflake" on the beginning of spring
A simple, safe, and splendid Winter Olympics was unveiled
Making Beijing the world's first dual Olympic city
Every wonderful moment captured the attention of the world
Behind the major challenge of guaranteeing transport services
BPTC was part of the wonderful event

Listen, the snowflake is cheering
For the pledges before the Beijing 2022 Winter Olympics
"To complete the transport support task of the Beijing 2022 Winter Olympics, as a 'capital bus driver', I pledge to..."
These drivers safeguarded the most beautiful scenery and did their best
Wang Lijun and Zhang Xinjing, the couple both serving the Summer and Winter Olympics
While in the same Olympic bubble, they never met each other
In the minds of BPTC employees, reunion meant working together
Listen, the snowflake is cheering for the spirit of the Winter Olympics
Although not an athlete, every BPTC employee
Has their role model
She is the torchbearer for the Beijing 2022 Winter Olympics
National model driver Chang Hongxia

At the opening ceremony, the national flag was passed on
Engaged in it was a driver serving at an altitude of more than 1,000 meters
He is Zhang Dehui, a driver suffering over 20 elbow injuries
We aspire to bring out the best of Beijing to the world
Tens of thousands of BPTC employees, thousands of vehicles, immediate operation control, zero errors
The spirit of the Winter Olympics has empowered our world-class passenger transport services
It is a brilliant achievement of BPTC

Listen, the snowflake is cheering
It is here to stay and turn into a torch

The new-era transport publicity competition

Scan the QR code to watch the *Listen the Snowflake is Cheering*

Transport Services for Major Events

With a strong sense of political responsibility and mission, we mobilize all employees to serve significant events such as the 20th CPC National Congress, the "two sessions", and the China International Fair for Trade in Services, with the highest standards, the strongest and most practical measures, and the best morale. We strengthen emergency handling and accomplish transport service tasks brilliantly. On special occasions such as the Spring Festival, National Day, and the back-to-school season, we also make plans in advance to meet the travel needs of passengers to the best of our ability.

261
Inspectors dispatched on average

2,380
Operating vehicles inspected every day

Case

Striving for excellence to ensure no mistakes during the "two sessions"

At 9:50 a.m. on March 3, 2022, as the G6732 train taken by the Hebei Provincial Delegation slowly entered Beijing West Railway Station, the transport task of the 2022 National People's Congress officially began. With national interests in mind, Beijing Beiqi Taxi Group Co., Ltd., a subsidiary of BPTC, adopted the highest standard and prepared careful plans in schedules, task assignments, personnel selection, vehicles, conduct and discipline, high-quality service, responsibility implementation, etc. During the "two sessions", the company ensured transport services for all 34 delegations and 20 local groups and military bands to the National People's Congress. A total of 6,103 trips were made, transporting 58,500 passengers and more than 12,000 pieces of luggage, covering a safe transport distance of 207,498 kilometers. It guaranteed transport safety, smooth vehicle operations, quality services, public order, and effective COVID-19 control. It is the 45th transport service it provided for the National People's Congress, securing satisfactory achievements on behalf of the people.

Serving the "two sessions"

Joint Fight Against COVID-19

United, we are sure to win. In the battle against COVID-19, our strongest support came from passengers and the most powerful force stemmed from the cooperation of each employee. In BPTC, we were convinced that by working together with passengers and employees could combine expedited and strict COVID-19 control measures with practical and detailed kindness to build a solid barrier against the virus.

1,151

Sub-routes adjusted temporarily to stop the spread of the virus

Pooling strengths together

Epidemic control is for everyone but also by everyone. In the critical period of COVID-19 fight, BPTC fulfilled the epidemic control responsibilities of the public transport industry to ensure that duties were implemented in every trip and link. We also updated COVID-19 measures as the situation evolved, striving to provide passengers with a safe environment.

Accurate and rapid response

Transport services during the COVID-19

Flexible emergency plans

From May to June 2022, to implement the requirements of the CPC Beijing Municipal Committee and Beijing Municipal People's Government to "suspend social activities and take decisive measures to quickly remove the risk of epidemic control", we acted swiftly and precisely and adopted temporary operation control measures in the southern part of Chaoyang District, and the entire region of Fangshan District, Shunyi District, Fengtai District, as well as other surrounding districts.

To complete the emergency transport task assigned by the Beijing government without errors, BPTC formulated the Emergency Transport Work Plan for Responding to COVID-19, established the emergency transport command center and frontline command of BPTC, and brought together 2,000 vehicles, 3,000 drivers, and more than 400 management and operation control personnel to form 18 emergency fleets, including nine emergency transport fleets and nine emergency backup fleets.

From November to December 2022, to implement the requirements of "no suspension of bus services, routes, and stations" and overcome the impact of COVID-19 measures on bus operations, BPTC formulated the *Ground Public Transport Work Plan Under the Rapid Development of COVID-19*, handled emergencies at bus depots and along routes, and made rational planning of transport capacity. These actions helped the capital to survive the first wave of infection peak and Beijing residents to move around the city.

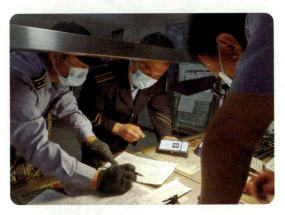

Bus drivers have their health codes checked

Bus depots carried out COVID-19 control

Implementing measures in detail

To prevent the barrier against COVID-19, BPTC insisted on implementing all COVID-19 measures strictly and meticulously, improved the prevention and control system, and carried out COVID-related risk investigations, COVID-19 prevention inspections, and emergency drills to keep the virus at bay.

Improving the epidemic control system

We formulated and updated various COVID-19 control documents in a timely manner and released COVID-19 response documents such as the COVID-19 Control Manual (Simplified) to improve the epidemic prevention system of the Corporation. We kept and improved the basic records of COVID-19 prevention information, which were updated in real-time as the epidemic developed.

Organizing inspections and drills

Through regular and special inspections, we got a thorough picture of how COVID-19 control measures were implemented in each subsidiary. We organized video simulations on the theme of "operating vehicles carrying passengers exposed to infection risks", strengthened prevention and control measures, and effectively improved emergency responses.

400+

COVID-19 control documents and notices formulated and issued

240

Daily reports on dynamic COVID-19 control information written

众志成城
抗疫情

Unity to combat COVID-19

Caring about employees

When combating COVID-19, we offered more care to employees and implemented employee support and care measures as required, so that BPTC's employees could continue to work without worries.

Epidemic control guarantee

- We kept a record of the vaccination and nucleic acid testing of bus attendants and strengthened the training of bus attendants on epidemic prevention and their performance.
- We adjusted the on-duty rate and shift type according to scientific instructions swiftly and maintained logistics support.

Employee care initiatives

- We cared about employees in need affected by COVID-19 and sent items such as disinfectant spray and rinse-free hand wash to employees.
- We cared about employees on the front line and the trade union sent them protective and daily necessities worth RMB 300 each person.

Science-based understanding of epidemic prevention

- We carried out epidemic prevention knowledge quizzes on the theme of "preventing COVID-19 reasonably and overcoming difficulties together", so that employees could master the knowledge and skills to fight the virus.
- We kept updated on employees' work from home, their life, and psychological well-being and provided employees with psychological counseling and Q&A services.

RMB
10,502,600
Worth of COVID-19 fund set up by trade unions at all levels in the Corporation

122,800
Employees covered by caring visits

RMB
4,342,200
Worth of donations or materials distributed

Delivering medical items to employees

Sending care to the employees responsible for transport tasks for the Xiaotangshan Fangcang shelter hospital

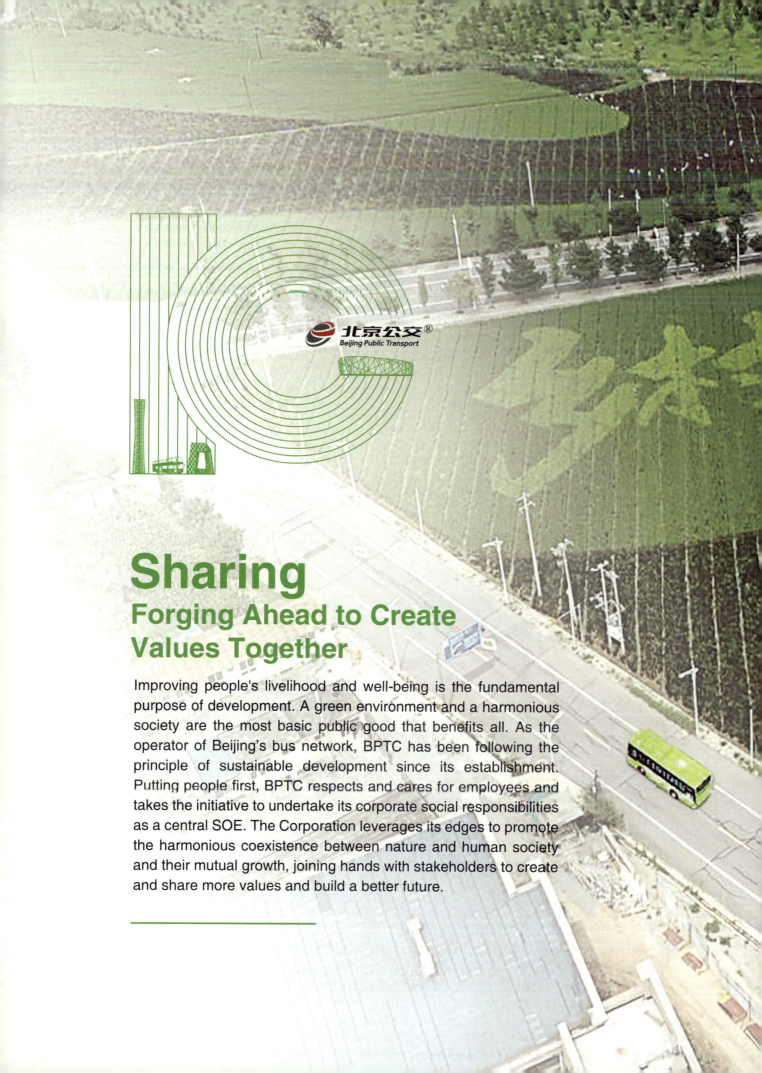

Sharing
Forging Ahead to Create Values Together

Improving people's livelihood and well-being is the fundamental purpose of development. A green environment and a harmonious society are the most basic public good that benefits all. As the operator of Beijing's bus network, BPTC has been following the principle of sustainable development since its establishment. Putting people first, BPTC respects and cares for employees and takes the initiative to undertake its corporate social responsibilities as a central SOE. The Corporation leverages its edges to promote the harmonious coexistence between nature and human society and their mutual growth, joining hands with stakeholders to create and share more values and build a better future.

Contribution to UN SDGs

Unleashing of the Full Potential of All Employees

Putting people first makes big things happen. The past century of BPTC records the contributions and forward progress of hard workers. We grow together with our employees and are committed to creating an equal, inclusive, and healthy career platform. We share our corporate achievement with our employees as it benefits from their unity and dedication. Meanwhile, we strive to enhance employees' sense of professional identity, gain, and well-being, give full play to their talents, and maximize their value, so that they can live wonderfully through hard work.

Working more decently

Employees are the mainstay for sustainable corporate development. In strict accordance with laws and regulations such as the *Labor Law of the People's Republic of China*, we provide equal employment opportunities and attractive remuneration and benefits for employees and protect their basic rights. We strive for unblocked communication channels for employees to make their opinions expressed and voices heard.

Diversity, equality, and inclusion

We keep a fair and open recruitment system and safeguard the basic rights of employees with a sound employment management system. The *BPTC Management Measures on Anti-Violence, Discrimination, and Sexual Harassment in Workplaces* is put in place to ensure an equal, safe, and healthy workplace.

Better compensation incentives

We provide five insurances (basic pension insurance, basic medical insurance, unemployment insurance, work injury insurance, and maternity insurance) and housing provident fund on time and in full for employees. We also improve our compensation and benefits system, reward mechanism, and annuity management to fully recognize the contributions of employees.

Democratic communication

We work to establish a sound mechanism for open and democratic management of enterprise affairs, and have convened the fourth and fifth sessions of the Third Worker Representative Congress, and further improved the working mechanism of employees serving as board directors and board supervisors. A public column was established at "Online Workers' Home" to unblock the channel to track employee demands.

Employees by gender

Female 25.43%

Male 74.57%

Employees by age group

51 years old or older 26.17%

30 years old or younger 2.61%

31-50 years old 71.22%

1,928
Jobs created

100%
Labor contract rate

100%
Social insurance coverage

11
Paid leaves per capita

40.5%
Percentage of female management

73.7%
Year-on-year increase of new hires with master's degrees or above

62.5%
Year-on-year increase of graduates from globally renowned universities and domestic top universities introduced

Accompanying employees to boost vitality

Regarding employees as a source of our lasting development, we develop together with our employees under the concept of "improving ourselves by helping others". We also vigorously promote pilot programs of building a country with strong transport network and the integration between industry and education. Meanwhile, we continue the lifelong vocational education project to cultivate highly skilled talents, and fully unleash potential and vitality of employees with stages for showcasing their talents.

Talent cultivation

Focusing on talent cultivation and the team building, we actively provide jobs, recruit college graduates, and introduce high-quality talents, along with the continuous promotion of talent "Navigation Plan" and management trainee projects. We have built a talent cultivation system with training from the source as the basis, training tracking as the means, and on-the-job training as the key, so as to comprehensively improve the quality and ability of talents.

Additionally, we plan to build a contingent of officials en bloc and have developed a training and utilization system from top to down with a virtuous cycle. We also implement several tasks, that are "Cornerstone Training", "Backbone Training", "Excellent Performer Training", and "Leader Training", to build a team of high-quality professional managers, vigorously cultivate excellent young officials, and provide platforms for talents to grow.

Employee training

We further improve the vocational education system. To support employee growth and career development from all aspects, we provide comprehensive empowerment training around all employee development stages, vigorously promote a lifelong skill training system, and expand learning and training channels with rich contents of skill training.

Case — Building a growth platform to cultivate highly skilled talents

In April 2022, to better build a team of skilled and leading talents, BPTC issued the *2022 Notice on the Recommendation of Technicians for Special Allowances of the People's Government of Beijing Municipality*. Participants were selected from outstanding technicians and senior ones in the front line of production and services, as well as leaders in Master of Skills Studios at the Corporation level or above. Reviewed by the Judging Committee, Cui Man from the Fifth Passenger Transport Branch and the other two BPTC employees stood out and won the honor of "Technician Enjoying Special Allowances of the People's Government of Beijing Municipality in 2022" together with other 61 technicians in Beijing.

Meanwhile, BPTC continues to pay more attention to and support skilled talents. We have revised the regulations on managing highly skilled talents, implemented the review mechanism for Master of Skills Studios, and dynamically managed the echelon of the studios. A dynamic management mode for studios was then formed, in which talents are prepared for both promotion and demotion, to stimulate the enthusiasm, initiative, and creativity of skilled talents and provide platforms for employee development and career success during their skill improvement and career development.

45
Young backbone trained in the Fourth "Ivy" Excellent Young Talent Training Camp

105
Training courses for Party members

29,000+
Trainees

140,000
Employees trained

4,806,505
Hours of training

81,551
Active users of "BPTC Online Class" APP

1,934
Drivers trained as apprentices in the new-type corporate apprenticeship training

17
Master of Skills studios at Corporation level and above

1
At the national level

5
At the municipal level in Beijing

11
At the group company level

Craftsman cultivation

We advocate and highly praise the spirit of craftsmanship. Craftsmen can fully shine on our broad stage through our innovative skill recognition, internal part-time lecturer training and certification, and an improved mechanism for the cultivation of highly skilled talents.

 Case **"Strong engine" of talents starts a new chapter for BPTC development**

In July 2022, BPTC launched the fourth micro-course contest for internal part-time lecturer training and certification during the "14th Five-Year Plan" period. After four days of course training and three days of project development, 101 trainees, combining their practical experience in their positions, understood the course positioning and learning objectives accurately and gained the ability to design and develop micro courses. They developed 101 courses independently and showed their outcomes through the micro-course contest in which 30 excellent students obtained the certificate of excellent lecturer. Talent cultivation lays the foundation for corporate development. This training certification is of great significance for building a model of being qualified for key positions, unblocking the learning and development paths of employees, and extracting excellent organizational experience. For BPTC, it is conducive to build an industry-leading training base with "abundantly qualified teachers, advanced facilities, lean management, and distinctive characteristics".

2022 Beijing Employee Vocational Skills Competition - Passenger Transport Drivers (For Buses)

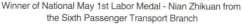

Winner of National May 1st Labor Medal - Nian Zhikuan from the Sixth Passenger Transport Branch

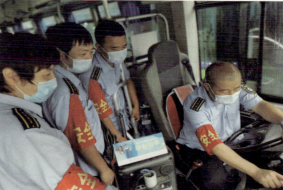

Hands-on training for a labor competition

Spotlight   Choosing a career and keeping to it the whole life

> I always hold the philosophy of "choosing a career and keeping to it the whole life" in my career. In the past twenty years together with BPTC, I did not only see its changes and development but also experience my own growth. I am truly aware of my progess having aligned with corporate development.
>
> —— Chang Hongxia, a driver of Route 1 of the First Fleet of the Fourth Passenger Transport Branch

I officially joined BPTC in 1995. From a passenger to a bus attendant, then to a driver, as days pass, I gradually grow and gain achievement. While training my driving skills, I am aware of the Corporation's support and assistance to employees in all aspects and my colleagues' persistent pursuit of dedication to work. More importantly, I personally realize that BPTC gradually stabilizes itself, develops and becomes stronger under the hard work of its employees, giving me a deep sense of identity and integration with BPTC's culture and atmosphere.

Over the years, steadily promoting the strategy of "making a talent-strong BPTC", the Corporation has integrated high-quality resources and industrial advantages to build a broader platform for employee growth. The most impressive for me is that I got ninth in the First Employee Vocational Skills Competition (For Buses) organized by the Beijing Federation of Trade Unions in 2010. The competition helped me improve my professional abilities rapidly and provided me with an important opportunity for my career. I was allowed not to comply with the requirements of working years and was promoted to a senior driver from an intermediate driver six years in advance, truly enjoying the dividends brought by BPTC's policy.

What BPTC has given to me is not only improved skills but also assistance in identifying my life positioning and a path to achieve self-worth. In 2009, I became the leader of "Hongxia Innovation Studio" in the fleet to lead studio members to tackle hot and difficult issues in production and operation. In the studio, we gather the intelligence and strength of our employees and showcase them, striving to bring more intelligent and humanized services to passengers. The fundamental driving force for our discovery and creation is our love and passion for public transport. We always have a sense of gain and happiness when seeing members show their innovative achievements in competitions and implement them in buses. I hope to drive more young employees to take the path of skills and innovation through this approach, allowing their talents to be fully unleashed and more creativity to flourish in buses.

The journey with BPTC is sweaty, but full of the most beautiful and unique sceneries. Today, same as my initial stay at BPTC, I hone my skills heartedly to provide the best service and bring all the skills I have learned into full play. In the future, I hope to witness more changes in urban landscapes and the continuation of good quality transport together with BPTC with my own experience.

Warming employees' hearts through sincere care

At BPTC, employees are our most important wealth. We keep focusing on and guaranteeing employees' physical and mental health and actively tackle their difficulties in their work and life. We organize abundant leisure activities and create a comfortable and pleasant working environment to help employees deeply feel our love and enhance their sense of well-being and belonging.

Employee health

We orderly promote the health checks of employees and organize health lectures and free medical diagnoses. Around the frequent occurrence of cardiovascular disease among employees, we have designed and launched the "Cardiovascular Special Health" service program to assist employees with major diseases in early examination and prevention. We also pay attention to the mental health of employees, carry out targeted psychological counseling, and survey the psychological suitability for all, to comprehensively protect their physical and mental health.

Mental health counseling for drivers for the Beijing 2022 Winter Olympics

Care and warmth

According to the assistance mechanism of "two guarantees and one reduction" for employees with difficulties, we carry out targeted visits, and launch summer and winter caring initiatives for on-the-job employees. Various heartwarming measures have passed love and care to all employees.

100% Physical examination coverage for employees

100 Trainees for EAP specialist training

6 On-site health lectures and free medical diagnoses organized

RMB 3.0315 million Funds to assist employees in need

860 Employees in need assisted

189 Workers' homes built

101 Relaxation rooms built

130 Workers' bookstores built

Summer caring activity

Winter caring activity

Diverse cultural and sports activities

We extensively organize a series of cultural and sports activities such as staff culture festivals, staff carnivals, and public transport markets, to cultivate employees' interests and hobbies, stimulate their vitality, and allow them to enjoy work and life with a relaxed and joyful mindset.

Fourth Staff Carnival

Diversified employee activities

BPTC market

Good Book Sharing Event

"Send You a Little Red Flower" activity

Cohesion by corporate culture

BPTC, with a history of one hundred years, holds its original aspiration of "Accompany You All The Way, Serve You Heart And Soul". Highly valuing the corporate culture, news promotion and brand building, we carry out online and offline publicity to display abundant cultural and creative products, and characteristic interactive activities to pass on stories about BPTC and promote our cultural brands. These provide a strong cultural impetus for the development plan implementation and high-quality development of the Corporation during the "14th Five-Year Plan" period.

Companionship culture performance in Lanzhou

Brand stop for companionship culture

BPTC Culture Manual

BPTC blind boxes

Scan to watch the "BPTC companionship culture performance in Lanzhou"

Spotlight · People hiding behind cameras

"What in cameras are exciting and moving moments, but efforts behind are always hard."

—— Wang Chao, a business supervisor of BPTC Publicity Department

Image is a solidified time imprint and a messenger that changes an instant into eternity. As a worker engaging in publicity, Wang Chao grows from a primary-level attendant, and knows that cameras are like a bridge, not only among passengers but among employees, and can be used for employees to better show themselves, helping more people see the different images of BPTC. He says so and does so. At BPTC, he is a recorder of transport services for major events, including the fight against COVID-19, the celebration of the 70th anniversary of the founding of the People's Republic of China, and the Beijing 2022. He is also a producer of videos played on buses as well as TV programs played in the staff lounge and operation control room. Outside BPTC, he is a contributor to the documentary A Hundred Years of Grand Line 1 directed by the Beijing Municipal Radio and Television Bureau, and the Reform of BPTC During the Past Century produced by the China Central Newsreel and Documentary Film Studio (Group). "During the Beijing 2022 Witer Olympics, I was lucky to climb the Haituo Mountain in the Yanqing competition zone. I was excited when I saw buses slowly driving on the winding road in the distance, with a background of ski slopes in the high mountain. I then quickly climbed onto the platform next to me and didn't have time to care that I almost fell. Back home, my face was itchy and painful, and I later learned that cold can cause peeling." Wang

Chao said. Whether carrying a camera, choosing a position, setting up the camera, finding an angle, changing the light, or switching a composition, all behind each scene and frame is long-time waiting and timely shutter pressing.

In February 2023, Wang Chao was honored with the nomination for the News Maker Award of the 9th "State-owned Enterprise Good News", fully recognizing his personal value and video and photography works. In the era of new media, countless people like Wang Chao have gradually become proficient in recording major events, speaking up for workers in public transport, and promoting corporate culture. Their constant love for public transport leads them to promote corporate culture wholeheartedly and convey more responsible brand images of BPTC.

Eco-Friendly Travel

In the context of China's 30•60 Decarbonization Goal (to peak carbon dioxide emissions by 2030 and achieve carbon neutrality by 2060), green travel becomes a consensus in the industry. Clear water, sky and air, singing birds, and fragrant flowers are not only people's wished living environment but profound practices from BPTC on green transportation and travel. BPTC adjusts its vehicle structure, saves energy, and reduces emissions to attract more citizens to take public transport, increasing the modal share. We also bring a cleaner travel environment and provide new green travel experiences, driving a sustainable future with green.

Greening the city by buses

We have gradually adjusted and optimized the energy structure of vehicles and vigorously promoted the use of pure electric vehicles and extended-range electric vehicles, to improve the efficiency of vehicle utilization and reduce inefficient and ineffective operation and resource consumption. Meanwhile, we improve the construction of supporting facilities such as charging piles and hydrogen refueling stations to enable every bus to travel through the city streets in a green way.

94.27%

Clean energy and new energy buses

217

Hydrogen fuel cell buses

2,220

New energy buses purchased

2

Hydrogen refueling stations built

1,524

Charging piles built in 225 bus depots

A hydrogen fuel cell bus

Case Operating new energy buses to promote a green city

With the purpose of speeding up the improvement of environmental and air quality, further enhancing the people's sense of happiness, and continuing to facilitate the battle of defending the blue sky, BPTC adjusts the energy structure of vehicles by introducing more new energy buses, such as hydrogen fuel cell buses. Compared with traditional buses, they are distinctive in appearance and structural design, with advantages such as smooth start, low noise and emissions, energy conservation, and environmental protection. They not only provide safe, green, and convenient travel services for passengers but make a more livable city.

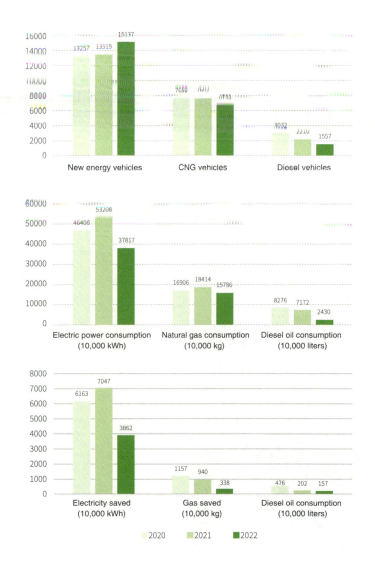

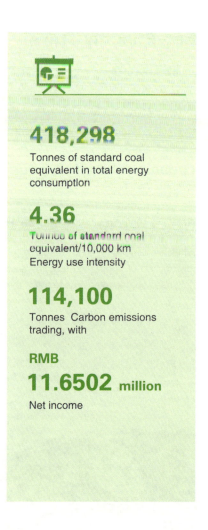

418,298
Tonnes of standard coal equivalent in total energy consumption

4.36
Tonnes of standard coal equivalent/10,000 km Energy use intensity

114,100
Tonnes Carbon emissions trading, with

RMB
11.6502 million
Net income

Maintaining a clear city and sky

We actively improve air quality in the capital by improving energy-saving and consumption-reduction management systems and establishing indicator systems for vehicle energy consumption. We also strictly control the exhaust emissions of operating vehicles and strengthen the governance and supervision of paint mist, wastewater, acid mist, dust, and other pollution. Vehicles are transformed towards zero emissions by recycling solid waste and gradually eliminating energy-intensive equipment, bringing a clearer sky to the capital with a more fresh and comfortable urban appearance.

Statistics of Discharge of Emissions (2020—2022)

Indicators(unit)	2020	2021	2022
Carbon emissions (10,000 tonnes)	275,587	288,376	246,261
CO_2 emissions (tonnes)	1,010,484	1,057,378	902,957
NO_x emissions reduction (tonnes)	186.25	123.41	57.05
Particulate emissions reduction (tonnes)	0.41	0.17	0.13
Hydrocarbon emissions reduction (tonnes)	40.93	80.78	30.72

Leading low-carbon travel

With detailed green actions, we broaden the scope of our environmental actions. Through waste sorting, green depots, green travel, etc., we actively publicize, advocate, and practice green development to develop low-carbon habits. Efforts are made to create a simple, moderate, green, and low-carbon social fashion and jointly guard the beautiful home with clear water and blue sky.

Promotion for green travel on a stop

4,256

Waste sorting training sessions, with

221,916

Trainees

100%

Rate of employees engaged in the activity of waste sorting in depots

277,500

Trees planted voluntarily

More promotion on green travel

We actively carry out activities such as green awareness month and public transport publicity week to promote new concepts of green travel, cultivate a green travel culture, and guide citizens to choose green and low-carbon travel methods.

Green depot construction

Our architectural design follows the Beijing two-star standard for green buildings. We use environmentally friendly materials and improve the energy efficiency of buildings. The construction of depots adopts dust reduction measures good for the environment like double spraying and wetting on working surfaces, as well as water-saving measures like secondary utilization of precipitation under ground.

Waste sorting

We actively implement waste sorting in all depots, establish management accounts, and create demonstration on domestic waste sorting to guide the staff to become promoters, guides, practitioners, and enablers.

Green office

We save every piece of paper, every kilowatt hour of electricity, every drop of water, and every grain. We take good care of supplies with less replacement, fully utilize recyclable resources, and keep offices clean with appropriate greening.

Touching Moments with Communities

Bus is good for people's livelihood. Committed to the spirit of "serving passengers heart and soul, taking pride in providing services, contributing sincerely to society and taking responsibility with courage", BPTC is working hard to take on and fulfill social responsibilities and carry forward civil convention. We strive to create sustainable supply chain and effective management, carry out regular voluntary activities of all kinds and gather charity forces to warm up the society, make happiness more accessible to communities and create more sustainable social values.

Retailing services at Chongwenmen bus station

Advocating responsible travel

Everyone is a responsible traveler. In order to build a more responsible and orderly travel environment, we carry out a special activity with the theme of "Responsible Driving and Pedestrians Going First", organize employees to engage in "My Commitment to Safe Driving" and "Going Home Safe with Responsible Travel" and jointly launch "Advocating Safe Riding and Fostering a New Paradigm for Responsible Travel", creating a bandwagon for responsible travel.

Responsible travel publicity

 Case Advocating safe riding and fostering a new paradigm for responsible travel

In August 2022, BPTC Training School held the "Advocating Safe Riding and Fostering a New Paradigm for Responsible Travel" event together with the Traffic Detachment of Daxing Branch of Beijing Municipal Public Security Bureau and the magazine *Motorcycle*. The 2022 Motorcycle Safe Driving Season and the "2022 Motorcycle Safe Driving Season Action" was officially launched to warn drivers to keep safe driving and raise the public awareness of travel safety.

Launching ceremony of "Advocating Safe Riding and Fostering a New Paradigm for Responsible Travel"

Case

"Responsible Driving and Pedestrians Going First" helps build a safe and smooth traffic environment in capital

On June 10, 2022, the Office of the Capital Spiritual Civilization Construction Committee worked with relevant units to hold the launching ceremony of "Responsible Driving and Pedestrians Going First-My Commitment to Safe Driving". Beijing Beiqi Taxi Group Co., Ltd showed up at a breakout session on behalf of the taxi industry. BPTC's drivers Liu Shaoshan and Jing Qingbo made a proposal and a commitment to observing traffic regulation and stopping at a zebra crossing, contributing to a responsible, safe and orderly traffic order in the capital.

Driver representatives made proposal and commitment

Building a sustainable supply chain

We make every effort to establish close, trusted and harmonious relations with suppliers, and continue to promote responsible procurement, improve supplier management system and enhance suppliers' CSR capability, aiming to build a sustainable supply chain that is trustworthy and compliant.

Supplier access and exit

- A sound supplier management system supports science-based supplier access and exit mechanism
- Strict procurement procedure and assessment mechanism minimize the adverse impact of external risks

Dynamic supplier management

- A supplier evaluation system is established to realize the dynamic assessment of suppliers
- Public bidding and selection help form a supplier pool

Supplier empowerment

- Regular business training for suppliers in supplier pool is held to evaluate their product and service quality and identify and address problems

Supplier management measures

Warming up the society with volunteer services

Public welfare is our friend. We shoulder social responsibility to give back to the society by assembling young volunteers to carry out regular volunteer services such as learning from the model soldier Lei Feng and bus stop pole and sign cleaning. Volunteers are also mobilized to respond to major events, gathering light and warmth of kindness to warm up the society.

Voluntary Services

BPTC "Model Couple" tie neighbors

Case

Chen Meng and Liu Ran are a post-80s couple working as drivers on Route 67 of the Third Passenger Transport Branch. They not only support and encourage each other in their work, but also are willing to give a helping hand in their lives. They are regularly engaged in volunteer services, bringing force the volunteer spirit of "dedication, friendship, mutual assistance and progress" with fortitude and resilience.

Chen Meng and Liu Ran are filial to the old and kind to their relatives. They often help the elderly in the community to move heavy things and take care of those who are physically challenged. Signing up as the first batch of waste sorting volunteers to clean up the community, they also try to acquire waste sorting knowledge on mobile APPs and through other platforms, and apply what they learn to answer the questions from community residents. In 2022, they participated in over 70 community volunteer services. They have provided 561 hours of services since they registered as volunteers in Beijing in 2018. The couple dedicate their life to stable urban operation and people's livelihood.

15,000+
Registered volunteers

200,000+
Volunteers on duty

52,000
Volunteer services

730,000
Cumulative volunteer service hours

New Hopes for Rural Vitalization

Committed to vitalizing the country with modern public transport, BPTC continues to strengthen daily coordination and overall planning, and consolidate and expand the achievements made in poverty alleviation in coordination with the extensive drive for rural vitalization. With more effective measures and greater strength, the Corporation aims to promote the efficiency and quality of the agricultural sector, make rural areas suitable to live and work in and ensure that farmers are affluent and well-off. Together with multiple parties, we strive to enrich villages on the new journey.

Aiding key areas by targeted assistance

We work to secure good performance in key tasks such as cooperation between the east and the west, paired assistance and regional cooperation, and intensify our efforts to offer support in industry development, consumption and employment based on our business realities, striving to consolidate and expand the achievements made in poverty alleviation in coordination with the extensive drive for rural vitalization in areas receiving our assistance.

RMB

1 million

Donated to industrial assistance projects in Inner Mongolia

RMB

8.62 million

Worth of agricultural and sideline products purchased from regions that receive paired assistance and just got out of poverty

RMB

30,000

Worth of COVID-19 preventive materials donated to Lhasa and Urumqi

1,601

Jobs created for rural workers from 22 central and western provinces

Donating anti-COVID-19 materials to Gaopu village

The Eighth Passenger Transport Branch buys agricultural products from Huanglingxi village for targeted assistance

Helping develop industries

We donated production equipment to the rural vitalization project in Oroqen Autonomous Banner, Hulun Buir, Inner Mongolia, one of the key counties to receive our assistance, aiming to improve the local agricultural support mechanism.

Boosting consumption

We led all subsidiaries to purchase agricultural and sideline products from economically underdeveloped areas that receive our assistance in Inner Mongolia, Hotan, Xinjiang and Lhasa, Tibet.

Promoting employment

The industrial assistance project in Tiedong village, Urubutie, Inner Mongolia, has brought jobs and more income for 50 local farmers.

We employed rural workers in 22 central and western provinces.

Improving education

Our technical school enrolled rural students from western provinces and offered them vocational education.

Donating materials

We donated COVID-19 preventive materials to economically underdeveloped areas in Lhasa and Urumqi to support the local battle against COVID-19.

311

Rural junior school graduates enrolled from eastern and western collaboration provinces in our technical school and offered academic and vocational education

20

Ex-service college graduates employed

236

Jobs created for rural migrant workers in Beijing

1

Senior administrative staff posted to Tibet among the tenth batch of assistance group in Beijing for the three-year paired assistance task

Supporting economically vulnerable villages

We work to consolidate the economy of three villages with weak collective economy in Zhaitang, Mentougou District, Beijing, and completed the first stage of the assistance task in advance, making strides in advancing rural vitalization and modernizing agriculture and the country.

Fulfilling the economic support task in advance

- We brought industrial support to Huanglingxi village and helped build a village history museum to boost local tourism

- We gave a Party lecture of "Learning Party history to vitalize the country" in Gaopu village and carried out a campaign to publicize local cultural tourism in the bus in Zhaitang

- We provided office supplies for the village committee of Facheng village and helped purchase Facheng honey and circulate idle farmhouses.

"Village Transport" project facilitates rural travel

- We built a bus stop in Gaopu village, which has a weak collective economy in Zhaitang, and integrated the New Gaopu Village Stop into 6 bus lines such as Route 892 to bring convenience to villagers in mountainous areas

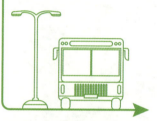

A new stop set-New Gaopu Village Stop

Helping to build Huanglingxi village history museum

Spotlight

Bus lines bring convenience to villagers

> Though the road is rugged and far away in rural area, we work to build bus lines to bring convenience to villagers, sending them hope and happiness.
>
> —— Yin Junhui, Deputy Manager of Operation Department, Eighth Passenger Transport Branch

Over the past ten years, BPTC has been expanding bus routes, stop coverage and service scale so that villagers can conveniently travel out of the mountains and citizens into picturesque mountains. The public transport contributes to agricultural product exporting, and the development of rural tourism, narrowing gap between rural and urban areas.

I am Yin Junhui from the Eighth Passenger Transport Branch and I am responsible for the "Village Transport" project from the design and planning to the opening of bus lines. Every BPTC employee knows the implementation of "Village Transport" project is very challenging. Most villages with new bus lines are of small population and surrounded by high mountains and steep roads. Some only have a dozen households and the roads to them are narrow and rugged, only allowing one small car to access, let alone large buses. In face of the challenging condition, we negotiated with governments at all levels to install protective guardrails on some rural roads and mobilized internal resources to rent more vehicles suitable for traveling in mountainous areas, so as to cover more villages with bus lines and improve rural public transport. In the meantime, we carried out investigations into villages and towns and held village-level symposiums to better understand villagers' needs and their travel habits, therefore localizing design for bus stops and lines.

The "Village Transport" project has not only satisfied the basic needs of rural residents, but also driven the development of mountainous areas in all aspects. Route Y16 has been extended to Hanjiachuan, which saw its first bus stop. Villagers of Hanjiachuan can travel to Yanqing urban area directly by bus, facilitating the travel of over 1,400 residents in 7 villages. At a small welcoming ceremony in Hanjiachuan, Zhao Yougang, Secretary of the Village Party Branch, said with great joy: "I am happy and excited today. From now on, we will no longer have to cram on the shuttle bus to go to Yongning and Yanqing urban area. It will be much more convenient for us to travel and our agricultural products like walnuts and chestnuts can be taken out and sold at good prices."

Today, BPTC is still committed to exploring more possibilities to serve people in mountainous areas with better travel experience and support rural vitalization. In November 2022, BPTC signed a strategic cooperation agreement with Beijing Branch of China Post Group Co., Ltd, hoping to enhance the terminal service capacity and build smooth two-way channels for manufactured goods going to the countryside and rural products going to city by leveraging resources including transportation capacity and sites, thereby making greater contributions to rural vitalization and spreading love in the mountainous areas.

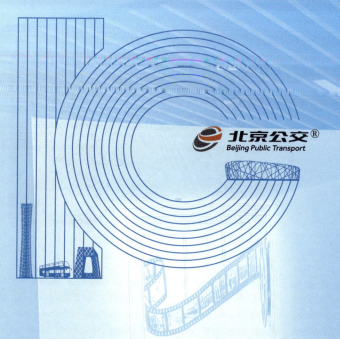

Prospect
Accompanying You All the Way
Towards a Sustainable Future

Embarking on a new journey towards the next century, we are preparing for the next stage. With the new blueprint for the Second Centenary Goal, BPTC strives to improve the well-being for the people as the vivid embodiment of its core value of "Putting people first, giving utmost care to passengers, promoting innovation and pursuing excellence". We closely follow the digital trends to promote the deep integration and wide application of modern information technology in all elements, every field and whole process of public transport. We will take advantage of the new infrastructure, pool advantageous industries and various innovative elements, and join hands with all parties to press on towards new goals, with an aim to turn the grand blueprints into better reality.

Contribution to UN SDGs

Better Transportation Dirven by Founding Missions

——Wang Hao, Former Director of the Ground Public
Transport Operation and Management Division of
the Beijing Municipal Commission of Transport

As the public transport service provider maintaining close contact with Beijing citizens, BPTC always actively responded to the questions presented by the times in the glorious centennial journey. Devoted to smart operation control, safe journey and transport services for major events, BPTC has made remarkable contributions to the public transport development of Beijing, regional economic and social development, and the implementation of the strategy of building China as a country with strong transportation network.

Wang Hao, Former Director of the Ground Public
Transport Operation and Management Division of
the Beijing Municipal Commission of Transport

Public transport in the capital city is the model for the whole country. Standing on the starting point of the new decade and the new century, BPTC should adhere to its original inspiration and live up to expectations, striving for the transformation into a modern comprehensive service provider of urban public transport with a broader vision and more effective measures.

Beijing Ground Public Transport Network Master Plan was officially released in 2020. Over the past three years, BPTC has optimized bus routes according to the requirements of the master plan, and the "3+1" bus route network system has taken shape. A range of effective measures were taken to boost metro connection bus services with remarkable results. In 2021, due to the COVID-19 impact, the passenger trips of public transport services declined, which requires BPTC to think over how to improve the service level and operation efficiency, strengthen publicity, and ensure passengers to have better experiences on riding buses, with the aim to boost the attractiveness of ground public transport services.

With the introduction of the China's "30•60" Decarbonization Goal (to peak carbon dioxide emission by 2030 and achieve carbon neutrality by 2060), the coordinated development of economy and environment has been elevated to a new height. Specifically for a capital city like Beijing, green development is essential to urban quality, the well-being of city dwellers, and the national image. Starting from 2012, BPTC has successively adopted less traditional fuel-powered buses in operation, and the bus models have gone through many upgrades to become more environmentally friendly with low-carbon emissions. Looking forward, it is necessary to further cut costs, reduce deadhead kilometers, develop charging facilities, and take combined measures to improve the quality and efficiency, so as to truly achieve green transformation.

Public transport involves multiple entities and many factors, and it is crucial and imperative to promote the comprehensive development in the field of transportation and to build a healthy and sustainable public transport ecosystem.

Recently, the radio program "Let's talk about traffic jams" jointly launched by the Beijing Municipal Commission of Transport and Beijing Traffic Radio was officially renamed "Let's talk about transport", which further highlights the necessity of integrated development of various means of passenger transport. In the future, BPTC needs to cooperate with multiple parties, strengthen communication, and complement each other, so that the development of various means of transportation can go hand in hand and promote the comprehensive management of the transportation field.

This year marks the tenth year since the first social responsibility report of BPTC was issued, which is a significant moment to commemorate. We hope that in the next decade, BPTC will be more proactive to promote the development of public transport industry for a better future through negotiation and cooperation with all stakeholders in flexible and diverse forms.

Towards a Better Future of Public Transport Side by Side

—— Arno Kerkhof, Head of Bus Transport Unit, UITP

The 2021 China (Beijing) International Public Transport Conference hosted by BPTC was held on November 12, 2021. At the conference, Mohamed Mezghani，Secretary General of UITP, praised that "Beijing Public Transport Corporation is a model for the Asia-Pacific region and even the entire world", and I fully agree with his remarks.

Arno Kerkhof, Head of Bus Transport Unit, UITP

On the journey of pursuing sustainable transport, BPTC has always been our closest partner and faithful supporter.

Since 2017, we have organized visiting groups to inspect the intelligent operation control system, in-motion charging trolley buses and charging piles and other facilities of BPTC. We witnessed BPTC's participation in multiple meetings, such as the International Bus Conference, and international seminars. In 2022, we signed a strategic cooperation framework agreement with BPTC and started the preparation for UITP Beijing Representative Office. This year, the new UITP Asia-Pacific director has taken office, and we look forward to joining hands with BPTC to strengthen connections with Chinese members and stakeholders of UITP and promoting the greener, safer and more high-efficient, intelligent and sustainable development of public transport. It is worthwhile to mention that BPTC has participated in the best practice project on global public transport network planning initiated by UITP Bus Committee, and displayed the multi-tiered network system of BPTC in the project results, which is an excellent example of network planning for mega-cities.

In the years of cooperation and exchanges, BPTC has always adhered to its responsibilities as a member of UITP Bus Committee and actively played a leading role in China to promote the sustainable development of the public transport sector.

Today, public transport sector priorities have changed. With the deteriorating climate change crisis, all public transport companies are faced with challenges such as improving urban environment and promoting the transition of urban mobility to public transport means. As far as I know, the current proportion of clean energy and new energy buses in BPTC has reached over 90%, which has made huge contribution to improving air quality and enhancing environmental benefits, and I think that is also the common goal for all public transport companies. As part of the public transport sector, we sincerely want cities to be cleaner, healthier and more livable.

In the future, we look forward to more and deeper exchanges and communication with BPTC to promote the mutual learning in international public transport policies, systems, rules, standards and technologies, making joint efforts to develop sustainable public transport system that are more state-of-art, energy-saving and environmental-friendly and people-oriented.

Urban Renewal to Revitalize "Old Places"

BPTC actively integrates into the new development paradigm of the capital. As Beijing boosts its efforts on urban renewal, BPTC rebuilds and renovates old bus depots to construct series parks such as the city smart space of "1921", through which we have achieved the quality and efficiency improvement of existing land resources, enriching urban service functions, and made contribution to the urban renewal of the capital.

Strengthening top-level design to integrate space resources.

To optimize the utilization of land resources, BPTC has moved large-scale parking, repair, maintenance and other functions out of the central urban area, and vacated a number of old bus depots carrying the cultural genes and historical functions of BPTC. At the same time, we put forward the idea of "using the space of bus depots to serve the functions of the capital and improve the urban quality", and develop project plans for the series of "1921" city smart space.

Improving mechanism to coordinate and advance implementation.

To speed up the implementation of the project, BPTC has put in place a task force for the city smart space of "1921" project to coordinate difficult problems and regularly schedule the progress of the project. BPTC Urban Renewal Operation and Management Co., Ltd. was established as a dedicated business entity that extends the functions of urban public services and facilitates the quality improvement and upgrading of industrial structure. The Beijing Urban Space Investment Management Co., Ltd. was also set up to take charge of the investment, construction and operation of pilot projects.

Accelerating construction process to shape a BPTC brand.

The Huayuan Hutong Park in Dongcheng District, which BPTC participated in the renovation, has been put into operation, transforming the old building courtyard into a modern and intelligent park with an occupancy rate of more than 90%. The park at Nanlishi Road was entirely renovated with a new academic architectural outer appearance; the design and planning of project at No. 3 Xinfeng Street has been completed and was included in the key urban renewal projects of Xicheng District.

A picture of the park at Huayuan Hutong   A picture of the park at Nanlishi Road

In the future, the "1921" series of parks will follow the gradual arrangement of "three steps for the entire project with biennium cycles" to advance the renewal and renovation in a planned and progressive manner. In this way, we strive to build a number of diversified public spaces that integrate public services, local culture and business scenarios, and build a featured brand for the urban renewal business of BPTC.

A New Highland for Standardization

In November 2022, the BPTC Standardization Pilot Project - "Beijing Ground Public Transport Operation Service Standardization Pilot Project" successfully passed the final assessment and acceptance with a high score of 97.5, which is a significant milestone in the development of public transport standardization in Beijing. The Beijing Municipal Commission of Transport and Beijing Municipal Administration for Market Regulation jointly issued administrative information which recognized BPTC's efforts on standardization. Standardization has been an important part in building modern public transport enterprises, and an important way to comprehensively improve management, service quality and service level. It plays a fundamental and leading role in promoting the modernization of corporate governance system and capacity.

As early as in the "12th Five-Year Plan" period, BPTC clearly proposed to move quickly in the direction of standardization, refinement, informatization and modernization. From March 2020 to March 2022, as the sixth batch pilot unit for national-level comprehensive standardization of social management and public service, we undertook the ground public transport operation service standardization pilot project in Beijing.

- -

We brave the important missions ahead with nothing to fear; we shoulder our responsibilities and implement them meticulously.

We focus on the goals and tasks of pilot standardization, adhere to the development principle of "standardization, digitalization and refinement", set high goals, and implement with high standards and high-efficiency. We strengthen the top-level design of standardization and set up a pilot leading group to coordinate and plan major matters for standardization development. We have issued the Implementation Plan for the Standardization Pilot Project to build the standard system of the Corporation. We gradually optimize the standardization work process and promote the coordinated development of standard mechanism, standard capability and standard culture. We also intensify our efforts in the publicity, implementation and evaluation of standards, change the "quasi-standardization" management mode of replacing standards with systems in the past, and achieve the dual standardization management of "form and essence". In this way, we have transformed our standardization work from empirical to professional, from partial standardization to holistic standardization. In the past three years, we have issued a total of 41 enterprise standards, 2 group standards, and revised 1 local standard of Beijing. In 2022, the public welfare subsidiaries of the Corporation saved RMB 545 million, overfulfilled the planned target, and improved the quality of bus operation control, services to major events, safety and stability, reform and innovation.

- -

The standardization work is an unceasing endeavor.

In the next three years, building a new pattern of "1+4+N" for BPTC's standardization development will be our overall work goal. We will focus on the two key areas of business operation and basic management, and improve the level of enterprise standard formulation. At the same time, we adhere to closed-loop management to create a sound environment of "rectification-implementation-improvement". Through strengthening coordinated cooperation, exchange and mutual learning, we strive to build the standard brand of BPTC, redouble our efforts to further broaden, deepen and elevate our standardization work, and make new contributions and achievements for the reform and development of the Corporation.

The final assessment meeting of Beijing Ground Public Transport Operation Service Standardization Pilot Project

Experts from the assessment team watch the on-site operation demonstration of the intelligent operation control system

A Pacemaker in Automated Driving

As the automotive industry gradually realize the deep integration with a new generation of information technology such as artificial intelligence, Internet of Things, and high-performance computing, automated driving has gradually become the direction of intelligent and networked development in the global automotive and transport fields.

In this wave of science and technology, BPTC actively focuses on the cutting-edge technology of automated driving and the strategic layout of next-generation intelligent transport, works out solutions for automated driving, and builds new growth drivers for its reform and development.

In August 2017, we cooperated with Mobileye Vision Technologies Ltd. to install the Advanced Driver Assistance System for four bus routes on a trial basis, promoting the transformation of buses from traditional passive safety technology to intelligent active safety technology. During the Beijing 2022, we cooperated with Toyota to pilot self-driving bus operation in Shougang Park from January to March 2022, which served 13,451 passengers with a total of 293 trips and 2,057 kilometers operated, accumulating experience in automated driving bus operation services. In November 2022, we joined hands with BAIC Foton, QCraft, Beijing Public Traffic Institute and other industry-university-research-application units to sign a five-party cooperation agreement, and completed the manufacture of an 8.5-meter-long prototype vehicle integrating the technologies of Connected Automated Vehicle Highway (CAVH) and individual vehicle intelligence. The increase in the body length, curb weight and gross weight of the vehicle demands more precise technical control. Thus, we have achieved a leapfrog improvement in the testing of automated driving bus services.

"Automated driving is the industry for the future, the embodiment of technology-enabled public transport, and the only way to build a modern public transport enterprise and achieve organizational innovation."

As Xu Zhengxiang, Head of the Strategy, Reform and Development Department, Secretary General of the High Level Autonomous Driving Demonstration Zone Special Working Group of BPTC, said, the fourth technological revolution represented by digital technology is unfolding around the world, and the development of automated driving is not only conducive to reducing the labor intensity of drivers and improving driving safety, but also creating immersive experience scenarios for passengers through the close matching of elements, such as people, vehicle, route and bus stop. In this way, we can improve the efficiency of public transport service, alleviate traffic congestion, and further contribute to boosting China's strength in transportation.

Looking into the future, we will seize the major opportunities of Beijing's high-level automated driving demonstration zone and intelligent networked urban road construction, work to establish a sound operation service mechanism, process and standard for automated driving, and continue to research and improve intelligent networked bus and automated driving solutions. Through accumulating resources in the field of automated driving, we will expand our industry influence, and gather strength to build a domestically leading and world-class modern comprehensive service provider of urban public transport.

Pilot self-driving bus operation in cooperation with Toyota

Training for the safety-driver of automated driving vehicles

Training for onboard attendants of automated driving vehicles

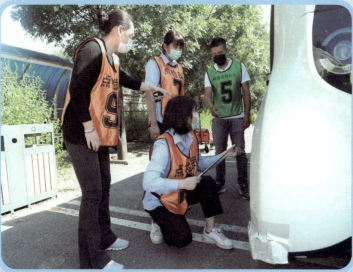

Training for spot inspectors of automated driving vehicles

An Innovative Think-Tank of Public Transport

Post-doctoral researchers are high-caliber talents with profound knowledge and exploration and innovation capabilities, providing important support for innovation-driven development strategy. Faced with the problems in the digital transformation and intelligent dispatching application of ground public transport, we follow the strategy on developing a quality workforce and successfully set up the first post-doctoral research station in the public transport industry in China in 2020, setting the precedent for industry peers. Building the post doctoral research station is of great strategic significance to BPTC. All BPTCers should strengthen their sense of responsibility and mission in improving the post-doctoral research station, and jointly build it into a world-class, innovative and high-end think tank of public transport with a global vision.

Innovative and sound institutional mechanisms attract talents and boost their vitality.

Over the last two years, we have gradually established and improved various systems and mechanisms for the post-doctoral research station, and recruited talents for multiple disciplines and fields. Focusing on the difficulties in corporate development, we have carried out post-doctoral research project management and initially established a database of planned research projects. At the same time, we actively communicated with post-doctoral mobile stations of universities such as Beihang University, Beijing Institute of Technology, Tongji University, and Xi'an Jiaotong University that are authorized to offer doctoral degree program for transportation, business administration, law disciplines. We extensively carried out the construction of joint training programs with universities, built sound research platform with abundant operation scenarios to attract excellent talents. In 2022, the post-doctoral research station received a total of 70 resumes, held 30 interviews with 41 candidates. Zheng Ying, a newly onboard post-doctoral researcher in 2022, mentioned: "BPTC has a rich range of application scenarios and accumulated massive data resources. As a postdoctoral workstation researcher, I hope to fully utilize the platform's advantages, organically combine theoretical foundations with actual public transport operations, conduct in-depth learning and research, strengthen practical innovation, promote the transformation of research achievements , and contribute to the high-quality development of BPTC. "BPTC made revolutionary attempts in digital informatization and automated driving, which drives me to study the impact on public transport policies and regulations by focusing on artificial intelligence and automated driving. I hope to conduct further research to promote the intelligent and standardized development of public transport." said Li Beini, a new postdoctoral researcher who was onboard in 2022.

A wealth of talent is vital to the success of a great cause.

As Xu Zhengxiang, Head of the Corporation's Strategy, Reform and Development Department and Secretary General of the post-doctoral research station, said, "The establishment of the post-doctoral research station offers the opportunity to carry out in-depth analysis of the difficulties and frontier development trends of public transport industry through the expansion of the ecosystem. It will summarize the fragmented experiences of the past into systematic theories and transform the traditional BPTC into an innovative enterprise." Embarking on the journey towards the next century, we will make full use of the advantages of the post-doctoral system, take this opportunity to strengthen areas of weakness, and let post-doctoral talents provide more effective support in enabling the transformation and upgrading and high-quality development of traditional public transport industry. At the same time, we will work with stakeholders to build a national demonstration base for industry-university-research-application collaborative innovations, expand the public transport ecosystem, and open new ground for talent development.

The first (expanded) meeting of BPTC management committee of the post-doctoral research station

BPTC senior managers met with the first-batch of post-doctoral researchers.

Sustainable BPTC for a Sustainable Future

Over the past century, the glorious lanterns created by our predecessors have illuminated the uphill battle we have fought, and BPTCers in the new era will carry forward the glorious legacy, continue to create sustainable value with sincerity, and draw up the blueprint for a sustainable future of public transport development.

Transport is an important sector which influences the global sustainable development, and sustainable transport is crucial to achieve the United Nations Sustainable Development Goals (UN SDGs). The SDG11 put forward that by 2030, all citizens will have access to safe, affordable, accessible and sustainable transport systems, which will be achieved by improving road safety and expanding public transport. But according to the Sustainable Development Goals Report 2022 issued by United Nations, SDG 11 pointed out "only about half the world's city dwellers have convenient access to public transport, and city governments still have a massive task ahead of them in seeking to enhance the availability and use of accessible, inclusive, safe, reliable and efficient public transport systems." Looking forward, the development of public transport is full of opportunities and challenges, which could either be stressful or transformed into source of motivation.

In the context of sustainable development, we closely benchmark against the UN SDGs, continuously enrich the connotations of urban mobility services, expand service scope and improve service capabilities. We constantly reflect about how to remain reliable and effective in the tide of development of our times, to carry forward the social responsibility legacy of "serving the people", and draw on our professional strengths to facilitate sustainable development with sustainable public transport.

CSR philosophy and contributions to SDGs

Public transport is for the cities and for the people. With the changes in Beijing's urban spatial structure and population structure, building an open and inclusive future public transport system will be the goal we continuously seek after. We will strive to strike a balance between "capital", "city" and "transport", as well as "relieving", "coordinated cooperation" and "breakthrough", actively integrate into the new development pattern of the capital, and make contribution to the construction of the Beijing-Tianjin-Hebei city clusters and the transit-oriented development (TOD) model. At the same time, we will continue to upgrade our own services and efficiently connect and integrate with other mobility services. On the basis of fully and accurately understanding the new trends and requirements of the people for convenience, diversity, accessibility, inclusiveness, comfort and safety, we will continue to deepen the supply-side structural reform of ground public transport, and offer a new comprehensive urban public transport service model where supply and demand boost each other.

The digital economy is driving the transformation of nearly all industries, and digitalization and intelligence will become the keys to the efficient and sustainable development of the future public transport system. We will push forward smart vehicles, intelligent management and intelligent operation control simultaneously and unleash the amplification and multiplier effects of digital transformation in all aspects of operation, management, and service fields. Relying on massive data, we can accurately look through operation status and passenger travel needs in real time, promote the continuous upgrading of public transport products and services, and realize technological empowerment, intelligent decision-making and precise policy implementation. In this way, we keep improving public transport operation efficiency, provide better services, and lead the innovative and sustainable development of the public transport industry.

Under the dual constraints of energy and climate, green travel and low-carbon transport will be the key to achieving China's "30•60" Decarbonization Goal, which will also be the main direction of future transport development, and under this trend, the dominant position of public transport in the urban mobility system will be further strengthened. As the main service provider of the capital's ground public transport, we will accelerate the construction of supporting facilities, reduce the consumption of fossil fuel such as gasoline and diesel while vigorously developing green and low-carbon equipment, transforming energy use mix, and speeding up vehicle upgrading. We promote clean operation, actively carry out energy conservation and emission reduction accounting and carbon emission trading, and show our support for low-carbon goals in a clearer and quantifiable manner. Meanwhile, we will improve the attractiveness and competitiveness of public transport, making the convenience of public transport meet people's expectations, effectively promoting the change of travel means of the people, and making public transport the first choice for people's travel, which will also be the focus of our future green public transport and contribution to green transportation.

We are fully aware that the future requires the joint efforts of all stakeholders, and we look forward to working with all stakeholders to jointly promote the in-depth development of China's transport industry.

Just as the road is always leading forward, we will keep pressing on towards the sustainable future.

Outlook

A hundred years ago, the bell of the tram vehicle indicates the establishment of BPTC. A hundred years later, the bell rings the same. BPTC forges ahead with firm steps in the new era to foresee the future. As demonstrated in the tenth CSR report, BPTC will work harder with stakeholders with its founding mission in mind to implement the guiding principles of the 20th CPC National Congress and grasp the strategic opportunities to address risks and challenges, blazing a new path for BPTC business with the highest standard.

Improving travel service quality to cater for passengers' needs.

We will practice the idea of "Mobility as Life" and advance the supply-side structural reform of bus operation to build a high-quality bus network system in Beijing. To ensure quality services, we will keep flexible and efficient operation control, provide real-time mobility information, and optimize the supply-side reform. We will innovate in our service mode to take account of the travel needs of different groups and develop diverse demand responsive bus lines. We will improve the water transport service of Baiyang Lake in Anxin County, Hebei and its water transport environment to put our water-bus services into operation in Baiyang Lake. We will make every effort to build brand lines and nourish brand value with cultural elements. We work to create an age-friendly travel environment and make public transport more inclusive. We will embrace the development philosophy of innovative, coordinated and shared growth and make use of depot resources to resolve livelihood problems such as parking and charging, thus benefiting the people with convenience.

Driving long-term innovation-driven growth with technologies.

We will make comprehensive plan for automated driving development approach in the public transport sector and engage ourselves in building Beijing into a high-level automated driving demonstration zone. We endeavor to develop new business patterns and technologies to underpin innovation-driven development. We work to unleash the power of digital transformation to promote the digitalization of public transport infrastructure, intelligentization of vehicle equipment and informatization of management system. By transforming "passenger, vehicle, route, networks, cloud and number" into the new driver for business reform and innovative development, we work to create a "Beijing template" for the digital transformation of public transport industry.

Enhancing core competitiveness based on talents.

We will strengthen the development strategy of making a talent-strong BPTC, expand the talent pool and build professional talent teams to foster new edges for high-quality development. Our post-doctoral research station serves as an innovation platform to cultivate interdisciplinary, strategic and high-level innovators with modern urban public transport philosophy and professional practices. We will strengthen education in Beijing Public Transport Senior Technical School to train and select skilled workers for main positions of public transport, delivering more public transport craftsmen to the society.

Fostering sound industrial ecology to contribute to industry development.

We will leverage industry leadership and adhere to the responsibility of scientific research. We strive to identify and address key and thorny industry challenges to tackle bottlenecks impeding industrial development, thereby boosting industrial growth with leading-edge technologies. Based on the principle of achieving shared growth through consultation and collaboration, we will work to develop domestic and international industrial ecologies, vitalize the entire industry chain and build a new public transport ecosystem of interconnectivity, collaboration, joint contribution and shared benefits.

Highlighting the value of public transport to respond to the call of the times.

We will develop a new paradigm for ground public transport where Beijing holds the strategic position and Beijing-Tianjin-Hebei conurbation develops in a coordinated way. We will strengthen the "Express by Public Transport" cooperation mode and ensure smooth travel for both passengers and goods to be delivered, better supporting rural vitalization. To contribute to China's "30·60" Decarbonization Goal, we will introduce the policy of public transport priority and low-carbon travel so that more people can choose public transport as an approach to green travel and increase the share of public transport in means of travel. We will establish an international exchange center to make BPTC brand go global.

We have embarked on a new journey of glorious dreams. Therefore, we will take firm steps together with our passengers and the time to become a domestically leading and world-class modern comprehensive service provider of urban public transport, creating a better future for public transport.

Key Performance

	Indicators(unit)	2020	2021	2022
Economic Performance	Revenue (RMB billion)	7.458	8.191	6.861
	Total assets (RMB billion)	65.179	64.521	64.327
	Net assets (RMB billion)	41.072	42.355	44.440
	Asset liability ratio (%)	36.99	32.08	30.92
	Total tax payment (RMB million)	340	415	289
	Number of operating vehicles	34,025	32,896	32,783
	Number of routes in operation	1,214	1,225	1,299
	Annual distance covered by buses and trolleybuses (billion kilometers)	1.068	1.139	9.84
	Annual passenger trips of buses and trolleybuses (billion)	1.826	2.296	1.726
	Response rate of complaints (%)	100	100	100
	Passenger satisfaction rate (%)	94.49	93.49	93.52
	Supplier audit coverage during the reporting period (%)	100	100	100
	Number of potential suppliers declined due to CSR non-compliance	0	1	0
	Number of suppliers terminated due to CSR non-compliance	1	1	0
	Number of CSR training sessions for suppliers	2	3	1

	Indicators(unit)	2020	2021	2022
Social Performance	Number of employees	92,264	89,014	84,211
	Labor contract rate (%)	100	100	100
	Social insurance coverage (%)	100	100	100
	Percentage of female employees (%)	28.33	26.49	25.43
	Percentage of female management (%)	39.34	39.30	40.54
	Number of annual paid leaves per capita per annum (days)	10	10	11
	Employee body-check coverage (%)	100	100	100
	Employee turnover (%)	2.50	1.73	1.86
	Workplace safety input (RMB billion)	2.330	2.408	2.164

Indicators(unit)		2020	2021	2022
Social Performance	Safety training coverage (%)	100	100	100
	Safety drill coverage (%)	100	100	100
	Traffic violation rate (%)	0.29	0.33	0.27
	Party A's liability accident death rate (passenger/million km)	0.00375	0.00307	0.0005
	Cumulative volunteer service hours (10,000 hours)	69	99	73
	Funds to assist employees in need (RMB 10,000)	190	209	303.15
	Number of employees in need assisted	989	1090	860
	Special assistance fund during COVID-19 (RMB 10,000)	858.40	-	434.22
	Number of people assisted during COVID-19	8,552	-	122,793

Indicators(unit)		2020	2021	2022
Environmental Performance	Number of obsolete vehicles	2,409	1,071	1,619
	Carbon emissions (tonnes)	275,587	288,376	246,261
	CO_2 emissions (tonnes)	1,010,484	1,057,378	902,957
	Percentage of non-fossil fuel energy (%)	13.20	14.40	15.92
	Percentage of public vehicles using new energy and clean energy (%)	87.34	91.06	94.27
	Gross annual energy consumption (tce)	477,415	495,424	418,298
	Energy consumption per unit of gross output value (tce/RMB 10,000)	0.25	0.24	0.20
	Natural gas consumption (10,000 kg)	16,906	18,414	15,786
	Electric power consumption (10,000 kWh)	46,406	53,208	37,817
	Diesel oil consumption (10,000 liters)	8,276	7,172	2,430
	Annual drinking water consumption (10,000m³)	202	263	208
	NO_x emissions reduction (tonnes)	186.25	123.41	57.05
	Particulate emissions reduction (tonnes)	0.41	0.17	0.13
	Hydrocarbon emissions reduction (tonnes)	40.93	80.78	30.72

Report Content Indicators

Contents		CASS-CSR 4.0 on Public Transport Industry	GRI Standards	Page Number
Cover Story				P1
Preface				P4-5
Message From the Senior Management		P2.1 P2.2 G3.1 G6.2	2-14 2-16 2-17 2-22	P6-7
About BPTC	Corporate Profile	P4.1 P4.3 P4.4	2-1 2-6 2-7	P8
	Companionship Culture	P4.1 G1.1	2-6	P9
	Organization Structure	P4.2	2-9	P10-11
	Corporate Governance	M1.1 M1.3 M1.4 M2.6 M3.1 M3.5 M3.6 S1.1 S1.2 S1.4	2-13 2-27 205-2	P12-15
CSR Management	Management Approach	G2.1 G2.2 G2.3 G3.1 G3.2 G3.3 G4.1	2-12 2-13	P16
	CSR Communication	G6.1 G6.2 G6.3 M3.4 M3.6	2-16 2-29 3-1 3-2 3-3	P16-19
	Highlights in 2022	P3.1	2-16	P20-21
	CSR Honors	A3		P22-23
A Decade: Seeking Innovation and Aiming High		M2.1 M2.4 M2.5 M2.7 M2.12 M2.16 M3.6	201-1	P24-43
Services: Taking Actions to Meet People's Needs	Urban Travel Facilitated by a Dense Network	M2.1 M2.2 M2.3	2-6	P46
	More Travel Choices	M2.1 M2.4 M2.5	413-1 413-2	P47
	Integrated Development Empowered by Public Transport	M2.1 S1.4	2-24	P47-49
	Digital Transformation for Smart Mobility	M2.1 M2.4 M2.5 M2.12 M3.6	2-6	P50
	Safety at Every Stop	S3.1 S3.2 S3.3 S3.4 S3.5 S3.6	403-2 403-7 416-1 416-2	P51-56
	Enjoyable Travel for Everyone	M2.3 M2.8 M2.9 M2.11 M2.13 M2.14 M2.15 M2.16 M2.18 M3.1	416-1	P57-59
Responsibility: Dedicating Ourselves to Bus Operations	Transport Services for Beijing 2022	M2.1 M2.12 S1.4	2-6	P62-63
	Transport Services for Major Events	M2.1 S1.4	2-6	P64
	Joint Fight Against COVID-19	S4.6 S4.10	413-1	P65-67
Sharing: Forging Ahead to Create Values Together	Unleashing of the Full Potential of All Employees	S2.1 S2.2 S2.3 S2.4 S2.5 S2.7 S2.8 S2.9 S2.10 S2.11 S2.13 S2.14 S2.15 S2.16 S2.17 S2.18 S2.20	2-7 2-19 401-1 401-2 403-1 403-2 403-3 403-5 403-6 403-7 404-2 405-1 407-1	P70-76
	Eco-Friendly Travel	E1.3 E1.6 E1.9 E1.11 E1.12 E2.1 E2.2 E2.3 E2.5 E2.6 E2.8 E2.9 E2.13 E2.15 E2.22 E2.24 E2.25 E3.1 E3.6	301-2 302-1 305-1 305-5 305-7 306-2 302-3 302-4 303-5	P77-79
	Touching Moments with Communities	S4.1 S4.2 S4.3 S4.4 S4.6 S4.8 S4.10 S4.11	203-1 413-1 413-2 414-1	P80-82
	New Hopes for Rural Vitalization	S4.5 S4.6 S4.8 S4.12 S4.13 S4.14	203-1 413-1	P83-85
Prospect: Accompanying You All the Way Towards a Sustainable Future		M2.1 M2.4 M2.5 M2.7 M2.12 M3.4 M3.6	2-16 203-1 302-4 413-1	P86-97
Outlook		M2.1 M3.6 S2.16 E1.7 A1	2-6 2-16	P98-99
Key Performance		S1.3	2-7 201-1 302-1 302-3 302-4 302-5 303-5 305-1 305-2 405-1	P100-101
Report Content Indicators		A5		P102
About This Report		A6	2-3 2-4	P103

About This Report

This is the 10th CSR report issued by Beijing Public Transport Corporation. We hope to disclose the Corporation's ideas, actions and achievements in sustainable development to stakeholders and make it a tool for deeper stakeholder communication and closer contacts and eventually for the sustainable development of the Corporation and society.

Reporting period

The report covers information about BPTC from January 1 to December 31, 2022. To enhance comparability of the data and continuity of the content, and the time effectiveness of publicity, some parts may cover information beyond the aforementioned scope.

New contents

The report has a new chapter entitled "A Decade: Seeking Innovation and Aiming High", which focuses on BPTC's CSR footprint in the past ten years covering the release of the 10th CSR report, the photo display reflecting the change of "transport services to major events, vehicles, networks and bus stops" and the reforms of key issues concerned by stakeholders.

Reporting scope

This report mainly discloses Beijing Public Transport Corporation's willingness, actions and performance in practicing sustainable development and fulfilling social responsibilities. For better expression and readability, Beijing Public Transport Corporation is also referred to as "BPTC", "the Corporation", and "We".

Data source

All data used in the report is from the Corporation's official documents and statistical reports. The quoted data is the finalized statistics. In case of any inconsistency between the financial data and those in the annual audit report, the annual audit report shall prevail. We guarantee that all data and contents have been reviewed by BPTC's management prior to the release of this report. We pledge that the report is free of false records, misleading statements or major omissions in the report, and we are responsible for the objectivity and authenticity of the data related to BPTC in this report.

Reference

The report is prepared in accordance *with Guidance on Social Responsibility (ISO 26000:2010)* issued by International Organization for Standardization (ISO), *GRI Sustainability Reporting Standards (GRI Standards)* issued by Global Sustainability Standards Board (GSSB), *The 2030 Agenda for Sustainable Development* of United Nations, Chinese national social responsibility standard, *Guidance on Corporate Social Responsibility Reporting* (GB/T 36001-2015), *Guidelines on Corporate Social Responsibility Reporting for Chinese Enterprises (CASS-CSR 4.0) on Public Transport* Industry issued by Chinese Academy of Social Sciences (CASS), which balance both national standards and international regulations.

Preparation process

Earlystage preparation	Writing	Review	Design and release	Feedback
• Set up a work group • Conduct peer-to-peer analysis • Collect information	• Confirm the report framework • Write the report	• Review the report • Finalize the report	• Conduct the report • Release the report	• Collect feedback • Work out further plans

Access to the report

This report is available in both Chinese and English versions. We provide printed forms, and you can purchase it online to get more information about our social responsibility performance.

Address: No. 29, Lianhuachi Xili, Fengtai District, Beijing.

Contact: Lan Yifan

Postal code: 100161

Tel: 0086-10-63960088

Scan the QR code and share your with feedback with us

金钥匙·SDG领跑企业
GoldenKey·SDG Forerunner

北京公共交通控股（集团）有限公司

可持续发展是破解全球性问题的"金钥匙"。贵公司积极行动，精准识别问题症结，以创新的解决方案突破问题难点，为实现联合国2030年可持续发展目标贡献力量，入选"金钥匙·SDG领跑企业"。

Sustainable development is the "golden key" to solve global problems. The company has been selected as "Golden Key-SDG Forerunner" for its proactive actions to accurately identify the problems and provide with innovative solutions to contribute to the achievement of the 2030 Sustainable Development Goals.

可持续发展 经济
CHINA SUSTAINABILITY TRIBUNE 导刊

图书在版编目（CIP）数据

北京公交社会责任报告.2022/北京公共交通控股（集团）有限公司编著.—北京：经济管理出版社，2023.10

ISBN 978-7-5096-9418-3

Ⅰ.①北 … Ⅱ.①北… Ⅲ.①公交公司—企业责任—研究报告—北京—2022 Ⅳ.①F512.71

中国国家版本馆 CIP 数据核字（2023）第 213988 号

责任编辑：张莉琼
责任印制：黄章平

出版发行：经济管理出版社
　　　　　（北京市海淀区北蜂窝 8 号中雅大厦 A 座 11 层　　100038）
网　　址：www.E-mp.com.cn
电　　话：（010）51915602
印　　刷：唐山玺诚印务有限公司
经　　销：新华书店
开　　本：889mm×1194mm/16
印　　张：13.5
字　　数：382 千字
版　　次：2023 年 12 月第 1 版　2023 年 12 月第 1 次印刷
书　　号：ISBN 978-7-5096-9418-3
定　　价：138.00 元（全二册）